First Things First

A comedy

Derek Benfield

Samuel French — London
www.samuelfrench-london.co.uk

CHARACTERS

Sarah, an appealing young lady with a romantic
imagination

Pete, a pleasant middle-aged man with a fondness for
marriage

Margot, a formidable possessive mother in her sixties

George, a good friend to have in a crisis

Jessica, an attractive wife with a secret or two

Alan, a good looking man in his forties with an eye or two
for a girl or two

These unlikely events take place in Pete's and Sarah's
house in the suburbs of a big city

ACT I   A Friday evening in the summer

ACT II   A few minutes later

Time—the present

Other plays by Derek Benfield
published by Samuel French Ltd

Anyone for Breakfast?
Bedside Manners
Beyond a Joke
A Bird in the Hand
Caught on the Hop
Don't Lose the Place!
Fish Out of Water
A Fly in the Ointment
Flying Feathers
Funny Business
In at the Deep End
In for the Kill
Look Who's Talking
Off the Hook!
Over my Dead Body
Panic Stations
Post Horn Gallop
Running Riot
Second Time Around
Touch and Go
Two and Two Together
Up and Running!
Wild Goose Chase

ACT I

The sitting-room of Pete's and Sarah's house in the suburbs of a big city

Nobody about. Then the telephone rings, abruptly. After a moment, Sarah runs in quickly and goes to answer it. She is a pretty, appealing young lady with a romantic imagination

Sarah Hallo? Ah—Isobel! *I* was just going to call *you!* I'm afraid something's happened and I won't be able to make it tonight. (*She sighs, regretfully*) Yes. I'm disappointed too. I was looking forward to it. But I— I had such a silly accident. I tripped and fell, and sprained my ankle. (*Suffering suitably*) Yes—it's agony! I can hardly put my foot down!

A car is heard pulling up outside. Sarah reacts to it and hastily ends her conversation

Sorry, Isobel—I'll have to talk to you later! Bye!

Sarah hangs up, looking a little shame-faced and runs quickly (and without difficulty) to the sofa. She lies down, puts her leg up and settles down with a magazine, the brave invalid

Pete walks in from the hall. He is a pleasant, attractive man in his middle years. He is carrying a wrapped bottle of wine, his laptop and the evening paper. He does not see Sarah, puts his things down, takes off his coat and goes back into the hall to hang it up. He returns at speed and stops, staring at Sarah in surprise

Pete *You*'re not supposed to be here!

Sarah looks up from her magazine, a little hurt

Sarah I *live* here.
Pete Yes, darling, I know you live here. But tonight I thought you were going to be elsewhere. So what are you doing over there?
Sarah I'm lying down. With my leg up. (*She resumes her reading*)
Pete I thought you'd be in the bath by now. (*He goes to sort out his things*)

Sarah Well. I'm not.
Pete No. I can see that. You're lying down. With your leg up.
Sarah Yes. Reading a magazine. (*She turns a page, elaborately*)
Pete Well, hadn't you better get a move on? You're due there soon.
Sarah (*calmly*) I can't get a move on.
Pete Why not?
Sarah Because plans have changed.
Pete (*returning to her*) You can't change plans at the last minute! Isobel's expecting you.
Sarah Yes. I know.
Pete So don't just lie there! Go and get dressed. (*He looks at his watch*) And perhaps you'd better cut the bath because there isn't time now.
Sarah I can't.
Pete Can't cut the bath?
Sarah Can't get dressed. (*She turns another page*)
Pete You know what Isobel's like. She does like you to make an effort.
Sarah (*suffering suitably*) I *can't* make an effort...!
Pete (*with a smile*) You're very defeatist tonight. Can't get dressed. Can't make an effort. You said you were looking forward to Isobel's party.
Sarah I was. But now I'm not going. (*She sulks a little*)
Pete You said you were going this morning. Darling, you fixed it weeks ago!
Sarah Well, now I've *un*fixed it.
Pete (*playfully*) I see. You're in one of your moods. Is that it?
Sarah What moods? I don't have moods.
Pete Yes, you do. You're in your sulking, sorry-for-yourself mood. All right—why aren't you going?
Sarah (*dramatically*) Because I've broken my leg!
Pete Oh, darling! You never said! (*He goes to her, sympathetically*)
Sarah You never asked.

Pete peers at her leg for a moment

Pete Where's the plaster?
Sarah There isn't any plaster.
Pete A broken leg and no plaster?
Sarah (*losing heart*) Well ... it's not exactly *broken*...
Pete (*with a smile*) I see. You're exaggerating. You're in your exaggerating mood as well as your sulky, sorry-for-yourself mood.
Sarah It's not my *leg* anyway! It's my *ankle*!
Pete Which one?
Sarah (*indicating*) This one! The one that isn't in contact with the floor!
Pete And you've broken it?
Sarah Well ... it's not exactly *broken*...

Pete So you haven't broken your leg and you haven't broken your ankle?
Sarah No... (*Defensively*) But I've *sprained* it! And that's why I can't go
to Isobel's party.
Pete But she's expecting you.
Sarah Not any more.
Pete She was this morning.
Sarah Well, she ... she rang me up. So I told her.
Pete You managed to reach the phone then?

Sarah avoids his eyes, guiltily

Sarah Mrs Trundle passed it to me.
Pete (*indicating the telephone*) And then put it back again.
Sarah Yes...
Pete (*peering at her ankle*) It doesn't look very swollen.
Sarah It soon will! In half an hour it'll be up like a balloon!
Pete (*alarmed at the prospect*) Really? Good lord...!
Sarah (*the drama queen*) I expected a bit of sympathy...
Pete Yes, of course you did, darling! I'm so sorry. (*He sits beside her, puts
her leg on to his lap, and smiles comfortingly*) There we are. That better?
Sarah (*uncertainly*) H'm...
Pete So—er—how did you do it, anyway?
Sarah Do what?
Pete Sprain your... (*He indicates her ankle*)
Sarah Ankle?
Pete Yes.

Sarah hesitates. Pete grins

You haven't forgotten, have you?
Sarah No, of course I haven't forgotten!
Pete So ... how did it happen?
Sarah I ... I tripped over the Hoover.

*Pete holds her look for a moment, finding this a little hard to understand. Then
he chuckles*

Pete You didn't, did you?
Sarah Yes.
Pete Tripped over the Hoover?
Sarah Yes!
Pete Why were you using the Hoover? We pay Mrs Trundle to do that.
Sarah I didn't say I was using it. It was there. And I tripped over it.

Pete So it was Mrs Trundle's fault? She went off and left the Hoover in the walking way.
Sarah No. It … it wasn't in the walking way.
Pete Where was it, then?

Sarah hesitates again

Sarah In the cupboard under the stairs.
Pete (*amused*) How did you trip over the Hoover when it was in the cupboard under the stairs?
Sarah I was looking for something!
Pete In the cupboard?
Sarah Yes. And it was right at the back and I couldn't reach it. So I moved the Hoover out of the cupboard so I *could* reach it. And while I was reaching it I … I forgot all about the Hoover. So when I turned to come out of the cupboard I… (*She peters out*)
Pete Tripped over the Hoover?
Sarah Yes… (*Defensively*) It's an easy thing to do!
Pete Had you been drinking?
Sarah Of course I hadn't been drinking! It was the middle of the afternoon.
Pete Well, I would have thought that a vacuum cleaner was rather a large item to trip over if you were sober.
Sarah I didn't notice it.
Pete Did you call the doctor?
Sarah No. Why?
Pete I just thought you might have wanted to get a professional opinion before deciding that it was sprained.
Sarah *I* should know if it's sprained or not! It is *my* ankle!
Pete Yes. Yes, I know it is, darling. A very nice ankle. (*He studies her very nice ankle for a moment*) Doesn't seem to be swelling up yet.
Sarah It soon will! It's only a matter of time. Aren't you going to offer me a whisky or something?
Pete You don't usually drink whisky.
Sarah And I don't usually sprain my ankle! It might have helped relieve the pain…!
Pete (*concerned*) Oh, darling—you never told me you were in pain…!
Sarah Of course I'm in pain!
Pete Right, then! Whisky it is. (*He gets up, carefully replacing her leg on the sofa, and goes to pour a whisky*) You should have said. You were being so brave I didn't realize that pain was on the agenda.
Sarah You don't mind, do you?
Pete About you drinking whisky? Of course not! Not if you're in pain.
Sarah About me not going to Isobel's!

Pete (*returning with the whisky*) Well, it does seem a pity not to go just because you've twisted your ankle. (*He hands the whisky to her*)

Sarah I haven't just twisted it! I've sprained it! (*She takes a generous sip, and reacts to its biting flavour*) You're trying to get rid of me, aren't you?

Pete Don't be daft! We've only been married six months. (*He chuckles and goes to unwrap the bottle of wine that he brought in*)

Sarah takes another generous sip of whisky and tries to appear casual

Sarah Are *you* doing anything special tonight?

Pete I'm not going to Isobel's party if that's what you mean!

Sarah So what *are* you doing, then?

Pete Oh—er—nothing, really.

Sarah You're not going out, then?

Pete No, no, I—I'm staying in, but——

Sarah Well, don't stay in on *my* account! (*She takes another swig of whisky*)

Pete (*a little surprised*) No. Right... (*He finishes unwrapping the bottle of wine*)

Sarah (*with great importance*) You've brought home a bottle of wine I see...

Pete Oh, this. Yes. I picked it up in Tesco's on my way.

Sarah We've got plenty of wine in the house already.

Pete Have we? Oh, well. Never mind, eh? The more the merrier. (*He laughs*)

Sarah But perhaps *that* bottle is a *special* bottle?

Pete (*looking at the bottle casually*) H'm. Yes. It *is* quite good, actually.

Sarah So what is it that makes you pick up a bottle of "quite good" wine from Tesco's and necessitates me being out tonight?

Pete I didn't say you had to be out——

Sarah Well, this morning over breakfast you kept asking if I was going to Isobel's party.

Pete (*returning to her*) I was showing interest, that's all.

Sarah You asked me three times!

Pete Did I? Well, that shows what a considerate husband I am. Always concerned for your welfare. (*Indicating her ankle*) Still doesn't seem to be swelling up...

Sarah It's bigger than it was! Soon it'll be *huge*!

Pete Really? Good lord...! (*He gives her ankle a doubtful look*) Feeling a bit better now though, I expect?

Sarah What?

Pete Your ankle! After the whisky. Must have made *some* difference, surely?

Sarah (*reluctantly*) Well—yes, I suppose it has ... a bit. But it hasn't gone completely!

Pete No, no. Still—that's a step in the right direction, isn't it? (*He smiles at her, optimistically*) Perhaps it was just a temporary twinge.

Sarah (*deeply affronted*) A temporary twinge?!
Pete Yes. Maybe the sprain has righted itself. Or perhaps it was just cramp.
Sarah It was not just cramp!
Pete Still, it would be a pity to miss Isobel's party if your ankle's feeling a bit better. Why don't we give it a try?
Sarah Give it a try?!
Pete Just a few steps around the sofa.
Sarah Around the sofa?!
Pete That's not very far. You're not doing the course at Aintree. (*Encouragingly*) Come on—up you get! You can do it! (*He starts to help her up*)

Sarah gives him a long-suffering look

Sarah I'm glad you're not in the medical profession. You wouldn't be famous for your bedside manner! (*Now she is on her feet*)
Pete There you are! Now you're upright.
Sarah I may be able to stand, but it doesn't mean that I can walk!
Pete You only have to walk slowly. Just one step at a time. See how you get on. OK? Right—off we go! Left, right! Left, right! Left, right!

With Pete supporting and assisting her, Sarah reluctantly takes a few unsteady steps, slowly at first and then gradually gathering speed as they circle the sofa like competitors in a three-legged race. Having achieved the objective, Sarah falls dramatically back on to the sofa. Pete smiles at her triumphantly

There! You see? I knew you could do it. So now you *can* go to Isobel's party!
Sarah (*glaring at him*) You *are* trying to get rid of me tonight, aren't you? I knew you were up to something!

The doorbell rings. Pete reacts in alarm

Pete There's the doorbell!
Sarah Yes.
Pete *Our* doorbell!
Sarah Well, don't sound so surprised. You must have heard it before.
Pete But I'm not expecting anyone! Not *now*...
Sarah (*immediately suspicious*) You mean you *are* expecting someone *later*?

The doorbell rings again

You'll have to answer it!

Pete Why?

Sarah Because it's my mother.

Pete (*wildly*) Your mother's not coming here! Not tonight! You were going out! What's your mother doing outside the front door?

Sarah Waiting for you to open it.

Pete But why is she out there?

Sarah Because I rang and told her about my injured ankle and she said she'd come over and bandage it. She used to be a surgeon. Or had you forgotten?

Pete You don't need a surgeon to bandage an ankle! I'm perfectly capable of bandaging my own wife's ankle.

Sarah Then why didn't you do it instead of dragging me to my feet and making me gallop around the sofa?

Pete You didn't exactly gallop.

The doorbell rings again

Sarah She's getting impatient.

Pete She always *is*...! (*He whispers*) Look—if we keep quiet she might go away.

Sarah Pete! She's my mother!

Pete Even so.

Sarah (*severely*) Go and answer the door.

Pete Yes. Right. (*He starts to go, then looks back at her*) But as soon as she's bandaged your ankle she's back on her bike!

Pete goes into the hall

Sarah remembers her whisky, thinks her mother might disapprove, finishes it off, gets up and runs quickly to put the glass down. Then she returns and settles herself on the sofa in suitably pathetic mode

Margot marches in, with Pete in her wake. She is a powerful, confident woman in her sixties. She sees her suffering daughter on the sofa, stops and gasps in a somewhat theatrical manner

Margot Sarah! You poor darling! (*She hastens across to her*)

Pete She's only sprained her ankle. There was no need for *you* to come charging over here.

Margot Charging? You make me sound like a bison.

Pete (*ruefully*) Yes...

Margot Let me see the extent of the damage. (*She examines Sarah's ankle*) Does that hurt?

Pete No.

Margot She can speak for herself! Sarah?

Sarah Well—just a little...

Margot (*to Pete*) You see? The poor girl is obviously in agony and putting a brave face on it. (*She continues her examination*) It doesn't appear to be broken...

Pete I told you it wasn't!

Margot (*looking at him, coldly*) I thought you were in advertising and therefore unfamiliar with medical matters?

Pete She's twisted her ankle, that's all!

Margot Typical male reaction. (*To Sarah*) I may have to prepare a poultice.

Pete She doesn't need a poultice! A couple of paracetamol and she'll be as right as rain. Then she can go off to Isobel's party as planned.

Margot Isobel?

Sarah Fortescue.

Margot (*ominously*) I've heard of *her*... (*She tries to recall*)

Sarah She was one of my bridesmaids.

Margot I knew it was something that I'd tried to put out of my mind...

Pete (*to Sarah*) Darling, Isobel will be very disappointed it you don't go.

Margot And *I* shall be disappointed if she does! It's out of the question. Bedrest is essential.

Pete Bedrest? For a sprained ankle?

Margot starts to sort out a bandage and scissors and things from her bag

Margot How did this unfortunate incident occur? Were you pursuing her?

Pete Of course I wasn't pursuing her! I was at work. She tripped over the Hoover.

Margot (*appalled*) The *Hoover*?! (*She looks at Sarah, inquiringly*)

Sarah Yes...

Margot Has Mrs Trundle tendered her resignation?

Pete No, no! Sarah wasn't *using* the Hoover at the time.

Margot I should hope not! Carpet-sweeping is the prerogative of Mrs Trundle. (*To Sarah*) If you weren't using the Hoover, how was it that you tripped over it?

Pete (*enthusiastically*) What a very good question! (*He grins at Sarah*)

Sarah What does it matter how I tripped over it? I thought you were here to give medical assistance, not to criticize me!

Pete Yes! If you're not going to help you may as well go home. (*He tries to urge her on her way*)

Margot I have no intention of going home until I have dealt with this emergency.

Pete It's not exactly a world-shattering event. It's a twisted ankle. (*Playfully*) Perhaps you'd better tell her how it happened, darling?

Sarah (*glaring at him*) It doesn't matter how it happened!

Pete Yes, it does! If your mother's going to give you the benefit of her medical expertise she'll need to know how you came to fall over a vacuum cleaner.

Margot I can only assume that Mrs Trundle had left it in the walking way.

Pete Oh, no. No. I don't *think* it was in the walking way, was it, darling?

Sarah gives him another severe look

Margot Then where was it?

Pete Where was it, darling?

Sarah (*inaudibly*) In the cupboard under the stairs...

Margot I can't hear you!

Sarah (*a fraction louder*) In the cupboard under the stairs...

Pete (*to Margot, helpfully*) In the cupboard under the stairs.

Margot How on earth could you fall over the Hoover when it was in a cupboard?

Sarah hesitates

Pete Shall *I* tell her, darling?

Sarah No!

Margot Ah! You were *hiding* in the cupboard! Just as I thought. (*To Pete*) You *were* pursuing her. And she sought refuge in a cupboard. I might have guessed.

Pete But *I* wasn't here, Margot, so if anyone was pursuing her it must have been the window cleaner. (*He glances at his watch*) Will you excuse me a minute? I need to make a quick phone call. Shan't be long!

Pete takes out his mobile as he darts out into the garden

Margot watches him go, balefully

Margot He was always very secretive. When I first set eyes on him I knew there was something secretive about him. (*She starts to bandage Sarah's ankle*) You're far too tolerant. You should listen to *me*—and learn!

Sarah But I *do* listen to you. And I *have* learned. (*Proudly*) And today I'm taking action!

Margot Not a moment too soon!

Sarah sets out her mounting suspicions stage by stage

Sarah After all, he does seem very keen for me to go to Isobel's party tonight...

Margot Exactly! Even though you're suffering under the burden of a physical handicap.

Sarah Over breakfast he asked me *three times* if I was going...

Margot Only a guilty man would ask a question three times.

Sarah (*delivering the coup de grâce*) He even brought home a bottle of "quite good" wine...

Margot Proof beyond doubt! He's got an assignation!

Sarah loses heart a little and tries to dismiss the idea

Sarah And yet he did say that he was staying in tonight...

Margot Staying in—but not necessarily alone! And then you tripped over the carpet sweeper and put the cat among the pigeons. So now he's gone to telephone whoever it is to prevent them arriving here when you were unexpectedly present!

Sarah That does seem to be the likely scenario. So perhaps I don't need to feel guilty...

Margot Guilty? *You*?

Sarah Yes. I'm afraid I have a confession to make. (*She plucks up courage, and confesses*) I didn't fall over the Hoover.

Margot smiles, delightedly

Margot I thought as much! I am an experienced physician and could detect no serious sign of damage. Clever girl! I'm proud of you!

Sarah (*losing heart again*) And yet I can't really believe that Pete would be unfaithful to me. Not so *soon*...

Margot There's only one way to find out.

Sarah Sorry?

Margot Put on a brave face and go to Isobel's party! I'll take you in my car. That's the way we'll find out what he's up to.

Sarah But if I'm at Isobel's party how will I know what he's up to?

Margot (*as if to a child*) You won't be at Isobel's party for long. We will return home early—and catch him in flagrante!

Sarah gives this a moment's thought

Sarah But if I *do* catch him in—er...

Margot Flagrante?

Sarah Yes. If I do—I shall have to divorce him...

Margot And about time, too!

Sarah But we've only been married six months...

Margot Six months too many! (*She packs up her scissors and things*) Quickly now! We must waste no more time.

Sarah (*surveying her bandage; bleakly*) But why do I need a bandage if I haven't really hurt my ankle?

Margot You are such an innocent! A stranger to deception. It is a most endearing quality. It is your bandaged foot that will help us to retain the initiative.

Sarah (*realizing*) Ah—yes—of course!

Pete enters from the garden, not looking too happy

Margot notices

Margot You seem a trifle downcast. Was your telephone call not a success?

Pete There was no reply. He must already be on his way.

Margot *He*? (*Aside to Sarah*) The situation is worse than we thought...!

Sarah *Who* must be on his way?

Pete (*reluctantly*) It's no good. I shall have to tell you. But it was *supposed* to be a secret...

Margot Married men shouldn't have secrets from their wives.

Pete Yes, Margot. I know.

Margot Especially if they've only been married six months!

Sarah *What* was supposed to be a secret?

Pete Well ... about George coming here tonight.

Sarah Coming *here*?

Pete Yes...

Margot *George*?!

Sarah He was Pete's best man, Mummy. Surely you remember?

Margot (*remembering*) Ah—yes. I remember his speech at the wedding. Far too flippant. And punctuated by vulgarity.

Sarah (*to Pete*) You mean *that* was why you didn't want me to be here tonight? Just because George was coming?

Pete Yes.

Margot So why did you have to telephone him if you were seeing him tonight?

Pete Because I wanted to put him off and arrange to see him tomorrow instead.

Sarah So it ... it was only *George* you were meeting tonight?

Pete Of course!

Margot A likely tale...!

Pete I'll try him again in a minute. He's never very far from his mobile.

Margot Well, you don't have to bother.

Pete I must! After all—tonight I must be here to look after my wife. (*He gazes at his wife with husbandly affection*)

Sarah (*deeply moved*) Oh, Pete...! (*Impulsively, she starts to get up to go to him, forgetting her injury*)

Margot hastily reminds her

Margot *Ankle...!*

Thus reminded, Sarah instantly limps, almost collapses, and is caught and supported by her mother. Pete goes to her, heavy with concern

Pete Perhaps you'd better go and lie down, darling. Rest your ankle. I'll make you some soup.
Margot Your soup will not be required.
Pete I make very good soup.
Margot Your brave little wife of six months has made a decision.
Pete Has she? (*To Sarah*) Have you? (*To Margot*) What decision?
Margot (*impressively*) She is going to Isobel's party.

Naturally, Pete is a little surprised by this volte-face

Pete But what about her ankle? You said bedrest was essential.
Margot She absolutely refuses.
Pete Refuses bedrest?
Margot You should be proud of her. She is determined—in spite of her injury—not to disappoint her friend. And *I* shall go with her.
Pete I didn't know you were invited.
Margot I *shall* be!
Pete Oh. Well—in that case... (*He cheers up*)
Margot You seem relieved to be rid of us.
Pete No! No—of course I'm not! Never! No! But if you *are* going I needn't put George off, need I?
Margot If it *is* George you're expecting...
Pete You've got a very suspicious mind, Margot!
Margot I shall just go into the kitchen and get some aspirin. (*She starts to go*)
Pete (*hopefully*) Oh, Margot! Do you have a headache?
Margot No, I do not! But your wife has injured her ankle and may require pain relief if the party should become boisterous.

Margot goes out to the kitchen

Sarah turns to Pete, rather puzzled

Sarah Why didn't you *tell* me that George was coming here tonight? I began to think that you were up to something.
Pete Yes, I know you did! But, you see—it was supposed to be a secret.
Sarah You shouldn't have secrets from your wife!

Pete I know. Margot *told* me! But this isn't *my* secret, it's *George*'s secret.

Sarah (*a little put out*) I thought George and I were friends. *Why* didn't he want me to know about his visit?

Pete I don't know. He didn't say. But he sounded in a bit of a state on the phone, so whatever it is that he wants to tell me about it's obviously a *personal* problem and I suppose he'd be embarrassed if *you* were here when he told me.

Sarah So *that* was why you asked me three times if I was going out tonight? So you could be sure that George could tell you all about — whatever it is — in private?

Pete Yes. Of course.

Sarah (*intrigued*) Do you think it's something strange?

Pete Oh, no. I shouldn't think so. George isn't a strange sort of person.

Sarah It must be pretty important, though, if he doesn't want *me* to know about it. Oh, dear—poor George...! Fancy having a problem like that...

Pete But we don't know what his problem *is* yet, do we?

Sarah No. But we can *imagine*...! (*She imagines, vividly*)

Margot enters from the kitchen with aspirins aloft

Margot Right, then! Come along, Sarah! Best foot forward! (*She helps Sarah to her feet*)

Pete Don't you mean *worst* foot forward? (*He laughs*)

Sarah looks back at Pete as she and her mother go

Sarah See you later, darling! Give my love to George. (*She remembers*) Oh, no! He mustn't know that *I* know he's here!

Margot looks puzzled, and supports Sarah as they go into the hall. Sarah limping extravagantly, Margot glaring back at Pete, suspiciously

Pete Have a good party!

Margot and Sarah disappear

Puzzled by this turn of events, Pete goes to the window to watch them departing. He waves, cheerily, and goes to pour himself a whisky

Outside, a car starts up

Pete notices that Sarah's glass is no longer beside the sofa where she had been sitting. He picks it up, puzzled as to how it got there. The doorbell rings

Pete puts down the whisky glass and goes out into the hall

Pete (*off*) George! Good to see you! Come on in!

George comes in from the hall. He is an agreeable man, not the sharpest knife in the drawer, but a good friend. Pete follows him in, anxiously

Did you *see* anyone outside?
George I saw an old lady helping an invalid into a car.
Pete Didn't you speak to them?
George I don't know any invalids.
Pete Yes, you do.
George Do I?
Pete It was Sarah!
George Your...?
Pete Wife. Yes!

George considers this for a moment

George I didn't know Sarah was lame. I've never noticed it before.
Pete She's never *been* lame before, you idiot!
George Oh, I see. A recent injury. It was lucky she didn't see me. You told me she'd be out tonight!
Pete She *is*. But she very nearly wasn't!
George (*puzzled*) Why was she limping?
Pete She fell over the Hoover and twisted her ankle.
George Ah! So now she's going to hospital?
Pete No. To a party.
George A party? You mean ... a sort of invalids' convention?
Pete No, no! An ordinary party.
George Won't she feel a bit out of place? Her being lame and all that.
Pete (*laughing*) They're friends of hers! I'm sure they'll accept her temporary immobility.
George Oh. That's all right, then. (*He smiles, happy for lame Sarah*)
Pete And the "old lady" was my mother-in-law.
George It wasn't!
Pete Yes. Sarah's mother. Margot.
George Oh, I've met *her*!
Pete Yes. She remembers! (*Going to George, sympathetically*) Oh, poor George... Here I am rattling on about my mother-in-law! (*He takes George by the shoulders, reassuringly*) I'm so sorry, old friend ...
George H'm?
Pete You poor old thing. Come and sit down. (*He assists George to the sofa and settles him down*) There! OK? Comfortable?

George is rather puzzled by Pete's consideration

George Yes. Fine, I have sat here before.
Pete I'll get you a drink. I expect you're dying for one! (*He goes to see to their drinks*)
George (*amused*) Well, not dying exactly. But it would be nice. I say—it was jolly lucky Sarah was able to go to a party after twisting her ankle. She might still have been here!
Pete Yes. It was a bit tricky. I must have banged on a bit about her going out tonight because she started to think that I was up to something! But you *had* said you didn't want her to *be* here.
George Well, yes! I didn't want *Sarah* to hear what it is I'm going to tell you!
Pete (*arriving with their drinks*) Here we are, then. You'll feel better for this.
George Thanks. (*He accepts his drink*) Well—cheers!
Pete Yes.

They drink. Pete sits and looks at George, waiting for him to start. But George remains silent

Come on, then, George! Your old friend is here to listen. Tell me what it's all about. (*With deep sympathy*) What *have* you been up to, you old bugger?
George (*puzzled*) Sorry?
Pete You sounded in a hell of a state on the phone!
George Well, yes—I *was*, actually. I still *am*!
Pete Well, there's no need to be embarrassed. Just—try to relax—and talk to me about it.
George Yes. I think I'd better. (*He takes a generous sip of his whisky*) You see—the thing is—I've got some news.
Pete So I gather! And presumably it's ... *bad* news?
George That depends on your point of view.
Pete Well—from *your* point of view.
George Oh, it doesn't matter from my point of view.
Pete Really? All right. From *any* point of view, then.
George Well, again—it depends.
Pete Depends on what?
George From which point of view you look at it. From one point of view it's good news. And from another point of view it's bad news. So it's a matter of getting the correct balance.
Pete And can we achieve that?
George Oh, it's not "*we*"!
Pete What is it, then?
George Well—*you*...
Pete (*humouring him*) All right, then—can *I* achieve this ... correct balance?

George That remains to be seen.

Pete tries to be patient

Pete George—are you going to get to the point?
George Yes. Right. You sure you're ready for this?
Pete I've been ready since breakfast! Anyway, I thought this was about *you*.
George (*thinking deeply*) I suppose you *could* pack up and go. Settle in the Seychelles? Change your identity.
Pete George—tell me what you're talking about!
George Yes. Right. Could I—er…? (*He indicates his now empty glass*)
Pete Yes—go on! Help yourself!

George gets up and goes to help himself to more whisky

George We're old friends, aren't we, Pete?
Pete Who?
George You and me.
Pete Of course we are! *Very* old friends. After all—you were my best man.
George Yes. I was, wasn't I? (*A beat*) Twice.
Pete (*laughing*) That's right! You did it so well the first time that naturally I asked you to do it the second time!

George resumes his seat, having replenished his drink

George Well, that's why I'm here.
Pete Because you've been my best man twice?
George Yes.
Pete That's not *bad* news!
George No. (*He sips his whisky*) Do you *remember* Jessica?
Pete Of course I remember Jessica! I was married to her, wasn't I?
George And she went mountain climbing.
Pete Yes. It was her hobby. I never fancied it myself. The Malvern Hills were good enough for me.
George The Himalayas.
Pete No, no—the Malvern Hills. Surely you——
George *Jessica* went to the Himalayas.
Pete Yes. I know.
George And never came back.
Pete I do remember, George… We went out there to try and find her. Searched everywhere. But there was no trace.
George No. It was as if she'd just … disappeared.
Pete Yes…

George So after a while it was assumed... (*He peters out*)
Pete I know what was assumed...
George And we had a memorial service.
Pete Naturally. We wanted to give her a good send-off. You made a speech, I remember. Very nice speech. One of your best. Very moving. I wore my dark suit and a black tie. And ... and cried, unashamedly.
George We *all* did...
Pete Yes...

A sad silence

George Well, we needn't have bothered.
Pete (*shocked*) George! What do you mean needn't have bothered?
George With the memorial service.
Pete It was our way of saying goodbye.
George Well, she's still alive.

Pete stares at him, in silent astonishment

Pete Still alive?!
George And kicking!
Pete Don't be silly. George! We gave her the last rites—*in absentia*, as it were. She disappeared on a mountain.
George They never found her body, though, did they?
Pete George—she fell off a mountain and we've never heard from her since!
George Well, we've heard from her now.
Pete Is this one of your jokes? You always did have a bleak sense of humour.
George It's not a joke.
Pete How do you know?
George Because I spoke to her.

Pete stares at him in disbelief

Pete You --- you *spoke* to Jessica?
George Yes.
Pete Have you been dabbling in the occult? Speaking to her through a medium?
George No. Through the telephone company. I answered the phone and it was her.
Pete She ... rang you up?!
George Yes.
Pete From the Himalayas?
George Pete—I thought she was dead! I was hardly going to ask where she was phoning from. I assumed she was somewhere handy.

Pete Well, what did she say to you?

George She said, "Is that you, George?" And I said, "Yes," and she said, "This is Jessica."

Pete And what did you say *then*?

George Well, naturally, I said ... "Jessica who?" I mean, I was hardly expected to know that *your* Jessica had turned up from the Himalayas after all this time.

Pete And she said it was *her*? *My* Jessica?

George Yes. (*He smiles*) "You were Pete's best man," she said to me. Well, I couldn't deny it, could I? I was rather touched. Fancy her remembering *me*...

Pete (*pacing; wildly*) There must be some mistake! It was probably one of your friends playing a practical joke. After all, you do have some very strange friends, don't you?

George (*calmly*) Well, we'll soon find out.

Pete How?

George She's coming here tonight.

Pete (*returning to him*) Coming *here*?!

George Well, I could hardly say you wouldn't want to see her, could I? After all this time.

Pete No wonder you didn't want Sarah to be here tonight! George—I'm married to someone else now. Did you tell her that?

George Of course I didn't tell her that! I could hardly get a call from someone I thought was dead and say, "Well, you've turned up too late because your husband's married someone else!"

Pete So she doesn't know?

George Of course she doesn't know!

Pete So she's going to turn up here—tonight—thinking she's still married to me?

George She *is* still married to you.

Pete But I'm married to Sarah now! You'll have to put her off!

George I can't do that!

Pete You'll have to! Tell her it's inconvenient.

George That wouldn't be much of a welcome, would it? After all, we gave her a good send-off. The least we can do is give her a good welcome home.

Pete But this isn't her home! It's *my* home—mine and Sarah's! Go on—ring her up and tell her! (*He pulls George up and starts to push him towards the telephone*)

George stands firm

George I can't.

Pete Why not?

George She didn't give me her number.

Pete Oh, my God...! (*He paces away*)

George I don't know what you're so worried about.

Pete You *don't*?!

George It could have been worse.

Pete How?

George Well, *Sarah* isn't here, is she? She's at a party with her mother and a lot of invalids.

Pete She very nearly wasn't!

George (*putting his arm around him, encouragingly*) Well, look on the positive side, then.

Pete I didn't know there *was* a positive side...!

George We can say hallo to Jessica—give her a glass of wine—catch up on old times—and she'll be gone out of your life again before Sarah and her mother get back.

Peter looks at him, doubtfully

Pete George—why is it that I don't believe you?

The doorbell rings

George That'll be her now!

Pete Oh, my God...! (*He abruptly pulls George down in front of the sofa*) If we keep quiet she'll think she's come to the wrong house and go away!

George We can't do that! It's a long way from the Himalayas. (*He scrambles to his feet*)

Pete (*looking up at him*) You said she was somewhere handy.

George But I don't know how *long* she's been somewhere handy, do I? She might have only just arrived. She might be tired after the journey and want to have a lie-down.

Pete (*getting up quickly*) She can't have a lie-down here! She should have stopped at an hotel if she wanted a lie-down.

George Don't you *want* to see her? Not even a little bit?

Pete hesitates for a moment

Pete Well ... yes, of course I want to see her... (*Quickly firming up*) But *you* can let her in! After all, it was you who invited her.

George Right! (*He starts to go, then stops and looks back at Pete*) Isn't this exciting?

George grins and goes into the hall

Pete is left alone, his feelings mixed. He tidies his clothes a little, as if wanting to create a good impression

Then Jessica comes in with George

Pete turns and they see each other. They hold their look for a moment, uncertainly

Jessica Pete...
Pete Jessica...
Jessica (*with a little smile*) Well, at least we remember each other's name.
Pete Yes...

They remain a few feet apart, just staring at each other. George finds that he is overcome by emotion

George It's no good—I knew I'd cry...! (*He takes out his handkerchief to cry into*)
Jessica Well, Pete? Aren't you going to embrace me?
Pete Oh. Yes. Right. Sorry.

So they embrace, she with a little more enthusiasm, but both fondly. And sincerely. And George cries even more! Pete extricates himself, not sure that embracing his first wife is a good idea, and gazes at her

Well ... this *is* a surprise...!
Jessica Yes. I'm sorry. It must be a bit of a shock for you.
Pete (*smiling*) Yes—just a bit! It ... it's good to see you again.
Jessica I expect you'd given me up by now?
Pete Well—yes! (*He laughs, nervously*)
George No, we hadn't!
Pete Hadn't we?

George glares at him

Ah—no! (*To Jessica*) No—of course we hadn't!
Jessica After all, eighteen months is a long time. Anything could have happened in eighteen months.
Pete Yes, it could...!
George (*to Peter*) Shall I get her a drink?
Pete (*blankly*) What?
Jessica Thank you, George. I thought he'd never ask. (*She grins at Pete*)
George Why don't we have champagne?

Pete Champagne?!

George Well, it is a special occasion, isn't it? It isn't every day that someone comes back from the dead.

Jessica (*appalled*) You didn't think I was *dead*, did you?

Pete Well—yes—that was what everybody assumed.

Jessica Oh, dear… How awful!

George You had a wonderful memorial service.

Jessica (*amused*) Did I?

Pete And George gave a very good speech.

Jessica Better than the one he gave at our wedding?

Pete Much better! He managed to omit the vulgarity.

George (*to Pete*) Er—*is* there any champagne?

Pete I don't know!

George I'll go and look in the fridge, shall I?

Pete Oh—yes—right.

George hastens out into the kitchen

Jessica (*with a smile*) He makes a wonderful best man.

Pete Yes. So … er … what happened, then? After you … fell off a mountain?

Jessica gazes at him in surprise

Jessica So *that*'s what happened!

Pete Yes. Well … that's what we all assumed. So—since then…? What have you been doing since then?

Jessica spreads her arms out, helplessly

Jessica I have no idea…!

Pete No idea?

Jessica No. It's all been a total blank. I have no memory at all of what happened in that time.

Pete No recollection of anything since the accident?

Jessica No. I suppose I must have been unconscious for ages…

Pete Good God…! How awful! I'm so sorry. (*He enfolds her in his arms, comfortingly*)

Jessica (*remaining there*) Then—all of a sudden—almost like a miracle—I was better! Fully conscious again!

Pete In hospital?

Jessica (*after a beat*) Yes!

Pete (*pulling back a little to look at her*) But still no recollection of what had happened in…?

Jessica No! Luckily, my long-term memory is as good as ever. I could remember everything from *before* I went climbing—you—George—and most importantly *our life* together! So I came back home as quickly as I could—and here I am! (*She embraces him, happily*)

Pete is a little taken aback by this scenario, and hesitates

You *are* pleased to see me, aren't you, darling?

Pete Yes! Yes, of course I am… It's just a bit unexpected, that's all.

Jessica Yes. I'm sorry. Never mind. You'll soon get used to the idea of having me home again. (*She drifts away a little, looking about*) It's a very nice house. When did we move *here*, then?

Pete Oh—er—this isn't *our* house!

Jessica Isn't it?

Pete No! This is *George*'s house!

Jessica *George*'s house? Oh, I see…! You—you don't mean you and George are … er…?

Pete No, we are not!

George enters with an open bottle of champagne and three glasses

George Here we are! Now we can have a proper celebration. (*He proceeds to pour the champagne*)

Jessica Pete and I were just saying how awful it is to have lost so much time together. We've got a lot of catching up to do.

Pete I thought you said you couldn't remember the past eighteen months.

Jessica No—sadly I can't. But you can tell me everything that's happened to *you* in that time. (*She smiles at him, sweetly*)

Pete Ah—yes—yes, I can, can't I?

George intervenes with the champagne

George Champagne! (*He hands the glasses around and prepares to make a speech*) Well, Jessica—I'd just like to say——

Pete You're not going to give one of your speeches, are you?

George (*persevering*) I'd just like to say—on behalf of Pete and myself— what a great pleasure it is to see you again, and to know that you're safe and sound and alive and well after the empty months that have passed. (*He raises his glass to Jessica*) Welcome home! (*He sees that Pete has not raised his glass*) Pete! (*He indicates for him to raise his glass*)

Pete Oh. Yes. (*He raises his glass, obediently*) Welcome home…

They drink

Jessica Thank you, George. That was very nice. I'm glad to see you haven't
lost your toastmaster's touch. (*She notices that they are all standing, rather
formally*) Well—er—shall we sit down?
Pete (*abruptly*) You're not staying, are you?

Naturally, Jessica is a little surprised and hurt by this

Jessica Pete…!
George (*glaring at him*) Of *course* she's staying!
Pete Is she?
George She's only just arrived! (*To Jessica*) Don't take any notice of him.
He's a bit nervous. (*He sits her down*)
Pete But someone might turn up! (*He looks at his watch*)
Jessica Oh, I'm sorry, George. Are you expecting someone?
George *Me*? No. (*To Pete*) I'm not expecting someone, am I?
Pete (*glaring at him*) Well, you never know! The neighbours might pop in,
mightn't they?
Jessica Oh, good! I'd like to meet your neighbours.
Pete No, you wouldn't…!
Jessica Why not? I'm sure they're very friendly. How long have you lived
here, George?

George looks at her in surprise

George Sorry?
Jessica In this house.
George *Me*?
Pete About six months, isn't it, George?
George (*blankly*) What?
Pete (*pointedly*) Since you came to live *here*!
George I'm not quite sure…
Pete George has lost all sense of time. (*He glances at his watch again*)
Jessica Why do you keep looking at your watch?
Pete I—I was just wondering how long a party would last … (*He looks at
George, anxiously*)
Jessica Oh, good! We're going to have a party to celebrate!
Pete No, no! Not *us*! Somebody else…!
George (*remembering, and smiling happily*) Ah—yes! Of course! The party
of invalids and old ladies!
Pete Exactly!
Jessica (*amused*) A party of invalids and old ladies? Isn't that rather unusual?
Pete It may be unusual in the Himalayas but it's very common around here!
How long do you think that sort of party would last, George?

George (*sagely*) Oh, I think it would probably go on for ages.
Pete (*aside*) I hope you're right…!
George (*thinking deeply*) After all, they won't be dashing about much, will they? I mean, there'll be no dancing. They'll do a lot of sitting down, I suppose. Sleeping, possibly. So the time will go rather slowly for them.
Pete You don't think that if they're just sitting about sleeping and not dancing they might get fed up and go home early?
George (*totally confident*) Oh, no! No chance!
Jessica Why on earth are you both so worried about a party of invalids and old ladies?
Pete We're very concerned about Care for the Elderly.

Now totally bewildered, Jessica wanders a little, looking about

Jessica You're very lucky having a house like this.

George remains silent, having forgotten that he now owns the house. Pete hastily alerts him

Pete George! Jessica's speaking to you!
George Is she?
Pete She said you're very lucky having a house like this. (*He nods, desperately, to remind him*)
George (*remembering*) Oh—yes—yes, I am, aren't I? I didn't think I'd be able to afford it. Not on the money *I* earn.
Pete You're far too modest.

Jessica has noticed a framed photograph of Sarah, which she picks up

Jessica What a lovely picture!
George Ah — yes — that's Sarah. (*He exchanges a quick look with Pete*) She's a … a relative.
Jessica What sort of relative?
George A very close one…!
Pete (*quickly*) She's George's wife!
George What?!
Jessica You're married now, then, George?
George Yes. Apparently…! (*He glares at Pete*)
Jessica That must have happened very recently.
Pete Yes, it *did*…! (*He grins at George*)
Jessica (*gazing at the photograph*) She's very pretty.
Pete (*enthusiastically*) Yes, she *is*, isn't she? He's a very lucky man. Aren't you, George?

Jessica How long have you been married, then?

George hesitates, briefly

George (*to Pete*) How long have I been married, then?
Jessica (*amused*) Surely you remember?
George Well, time passes so quickly when you're married. Doesn't it, Pete?

Pete glares at him

Jessica And was Pete your best man?
George (*to Pete*) Were you my best man?
Pete Of course I was, you fool! (*To Jessica*) It was only right that *I* should do it for *him*. After all, *he* did it for *me*.
George (*aside*) Yes—twice…!

Pete glares at him

Jessica (*to George*) Do you have any children?
George Who?
Jessica You and Sarah, of course!
George Oh. Er—I can't remember.
Jessica (*laughing*) Can't remember?!
George (*turning to Pete*) Do Sarah and I have any children?
Pete Not that I know of…!
George (*to Jessica*) Not that we know of. (*With a helpful smile*) But we have been trying!

Pete gives him a weary look and goes to Jessica

Pete Look, Jessica—I don't want to seem rude, and of course I'm delighted that you're still alive and kicking—but it has been a bit of a surprise, you turning up out of the blue like this. So perhaps we could meet up *tomorrow* and talk things over then?
Jessica (*sulking, suitably*) Oh… Why not tonight? I thought we'd be celebrating. (*She takes his arm and smiles encouragingly*) Consummating our reunion…
Pete Ah—yes—well, tonight's not very convenient for consummation. Is it, George?
George Depends how long a party lasts.
Pete And I am still in a state of shock. Aren't I, George?
George You certainly are…!
Pete Anyway, it doesn't seem very suitable talking things over here in *George*'s house, does it?

Jessica We won't just be talking, darling.
Pete (*nervously*) Won't we?
Jessica Of course not! So why don't we go back to *our* house and leave
George here in *his* house? After all, Sarah will be back home soon, won't
she?
Pete Yes, I'm afraid so…!
Jessica What?
Pete Yes, I should *think* so!
Jessica And then we can be on our own—just the two of us—as we used
to be?
Pete Ah—yes—I do see what you mean, but actually——
Jessica Whereabouts do we live now?

Pete remains motionless. And silent

George Pete…?
Pete What?
George Jessica's talking to you.
Pete Yes, I know…!
George She wants to know where you live now.
Jessica I rang our *old* number, of course, before I rang George. But whoever
answered the phone said that we'd moved.
Pete Moved? Ah. Yes. We have. *I* have! *I've* moved.
Jessica So where have you moved *to*?
Pete Yes. Now where have I moved *to*…?

George comes to his aid

George Highgate Road.
Pete (*gratefully*) Yes—that's it! Highgate Road. I'd forgotten for a minute.
I haven't been there very long. Nice little house. Isn't it, George?
George Well, *I* like it…
Jessica That's settled, then—we'll go there!
Pete What?!
Jessica I'll just go and tidy myself up a bit. (*She starts to go*)
Pete You don't have to do that! It's only going to be you and me. And *I've*
seen you already.
Jessica But it's been a long journey and I want to freshen up. Which way is
the bathroom?

Pete is about to tell her, then remembers that he doesn't live here any more

Pete George…?

George H'm?
Pete Which way is the bathroom?
George Ah—now let's see… (*He looks to Pete for guidance*)

Pete, his back to Jessica, mouths silently, "First left, then second right" as George speaks

First left, then second right.
Jessica Thank you, George!

Jessica sails out to the bathroom

George goes to Pete, angrily

George What the hell are you playing at?
Pete (*innocently*) What?
George Telling her that this is *my* house and that *I'm* married to Sarah.
Pete You could do worse.
George Why didn't you tell her straight away that you'd married again?
Pete I couldn't do that! The poor girl fell off a mountain and lost her memory. She's come back expecting everything to be as it was.
George Well, it isn't! And it can't be!
Pete George, you've got to ease into these things. You can't go at it like a bull in a china shop. I'll tell her. But in my own time. I'm not completely insensitive, you know. (*He pours himself a little more champagne*)

George sits down and looks at Pete, quizzically

George So … how do you feel about it, then?
Pete Feel about what?
George About Jessica. About … seeing her again. Does it … feel the same?
Pete In what way?
George Well … you did fancy her, didn't you? Years ago.
Pete Of course I fancied her! I married her, didn't I?
George So does it … feel the same?

Pete sits down, and thinks about this for a moment

Pete Well … yes. Yes, I … I suppose it does.
George Even though you haven't seen her for a while?
Pete H'm. Yes. Even though I haven't seen her for a while…

A moment's silence as they consider the ramifications of this

George So ... given the choice ... which wife would you prefer?

Pete I can't pick and choose!

George Why not? They both think you're married to them. (*He has a sudden thought*) I say! Perhaps you could keep them *both* on the go?

Pete George!

George You could keep one in your house and one in mine and dart backwards and forwards between the two! (*He laughs at the prospect*)

Pete gets up, decisively, and puts down his glass

Pete Right! Come on, then! Give me your key.

George (*shocked*) You're not *really* going to do it?

Pete Of course I'm not, you fool! But I've got to get Jessica out of here. If Sarah gets back and sees her she's bound to ask questions.

George I wouldn't be surprised...!

Pete So come on, then! It *was* your idea.

George Oh. Yes. Right. (*He digs in his pocket and hands over his latchkey*)

Pete Thanks, George! You're a pal! (*He puts the key in his pocket*)

George Wait a minute, though...

Pete Now what?

George Sarah and her mother can't get back from their party and find *me* here! So I'd better come with you and Jessica. (*He prepares to leave*)

Pete (*as if to a child*) No, George... You told Jessica that your house is *my* house.

George Only because *you* told her that *this* house is my house!

Pete Yes. So Jessica will be expecting you to stay here in *your* house, won't she?

George But what are Sarah and her mother going to say when they get back and find *me* here?

Pete Well, you *won't* be here, will you?

George (*puzzled*) You just said that Jessica will be expecting me to be!

Pete Yes, that's what Jessica will expect, but by then she won't *be* here, will she? She'll be at your house with me.

George (*realization dawning*) Ah! So I'm not *really* living here?

Pete Of course you're not, you fool! That's only the situation as it appears to Jessica. Do try to remember the plot. When you're speaking to Jessica, this is *your* house. Right? But when you're speaking to Sarah and her mother, it's *my* house. George, it's perfectly simple!

George (*trying hard to remember*) Yes. Right... When I'm speaking to Jessica this is *my* house... (*A beat*) So once you and Jessica have gone to *my* house I don't have to stay here in *your* house?

Pete Of course not!

George But if you and Jessica are in *my* house ... where am *I* going to go?

Pete You've got *other* friends, haven't you?
George (*uncertainly*) Yes, I suppose so…
Pete So you can visit them.
George Ah. Yes. Right. (*A beat*) Or go to the cinema?
Pete Anything you like!

A moment. But George is not satisfied

George But what do I tell Sarah and her mother if they get back before I've gone to the cinema and ask where *you* are?
Pete But they won't! You said the party would go on for ages because there'd be no dancing. Remember?
George (*remembering*) Ah—yes. (*He ponders for a moment*) So how long do you think you'll be at *my* house with Jessica?
Pete Does it matter?
George Well, it may be a very short film. So how long before I can get back into my house?
Pete *I* don't know! It depends how long it takes.
George To do what?

Pete glances, nervously, towards the bathroom and lowers his voice

Pete To tell Jessica that now I'm married to Sarah!
George Won't she be a bit confused? You've just told her that *I*'m married to Sarah.
Pete Yes, but I didn't know then that I was going to your house with Jessica, did I?
George Ah—no. *Or* that she expects to consummate your reunion.
Pete Exactly! So now I've got to tell her the truth, haven't I?
George Yes. I see… (*He contemplates*)
Pete And going to your house will give me time to … to work up to it gradually. I'll give her a couple of drinks and—you do have drinks in your house, don't you?
George Oh, yes.
Pete Good. So I'll give her a couple of drinks—and a bit of a chat—and then I'll tell her.
George And then she'll kill you.
Pete No, no! She'll understand. She's a very understanding woman. She'll be sorry, naturally, but she won't hold it against me.
George (*hopefully*) Ah! So you think she'll just turn around and go back to the Himalayas?
Pete She might. Anyway, after I've told her I'll come back here.
George After you've told her you won't be in a fit state to come back here!

Jessica enters from the bathroom

Jessica Very nice bathroom.

Silence

Pete George...!
George What?
Pete Jessica's admiring your bathroom.
George Oh—yes—good. Glad you like it.
Jessica Quite a coincidence, too.
George What is?
Jessica You've got a dressing-gown just like Pete's.
George H-have I?
Jessica Well, I presume it is *your* dressing-gown hanging up in the
bathroom?
George I'm not sure...
Jessica Blue and white!
George (*catching Pete's desperate look*) Ah—yes! That's mine.
Jessica Pete used to have one just like it.
George (*aside*) He still has...!
Jessica (*to Pete*) Shall we go, then, darling?
Pete Yes—I think we'd better...!
Jessica After all, eighteen months is a long time without.
Pete (*nervously*) Without?
Jessica (*taking his arm; sexily*) Without seeing each other, darling. All that
lost time to make up for—just think of it!
Pete I don't *want* to think of it...!
Jessica (*firmly*) Yes, you do! (*She pulls him towards the hall, hopefully*)
George Ah! Before you go...

Jessica and Pete put on the brakes

Pete (*impatiently*) What *is* it, George? Jessica and I have got to get out of
here!
Jessica Not *got* to, darling! *Want* to... (*She smiles, encouragingly*)
Pete (*laughing, nervously*) Yes—of course—*want* to... (*To George*) *Well*?
George (*profoundly*) I just wanted Jessica to know that after *you*'ve both
gone to *your* house—*I* shall be staying *here*—in *my* house. (*He smiles,
contentedly*)

Jessica and Pete look at him in some surprise

Jessica Yes, of course you will, George. This is where you live!

George Yes—I know! That's why *I* shall still *be* here even though *you're not* here. (*He smiles, proudly, at Pete, confident that he has mastered the plot as requested*)
Pete (*glaring at him*) But you don't have to *stay* here!
George I do when I'm speaking to Jessica… (*He nods, knowingly*)

Jessica looks puzzled

Pete I thought you were going to the cinema!
George (*with a shrug*) I may change my mind.
Pete But you can still go *out* if you want to and get a take-away!
George Ah—right! Good idea! I am rather hungry.
Pete (*to Jessica*) Come on, then—off we go!

They start to go again

George Chinese or Indian?

Once more Pete and Jessica put on the brakes

Pete That's up to you, isn't it!
George I'm not sure which I prefer… (*He tries hard to decide*)
Jessica (*helpfully*) *I* prefer Indian.
George Do you? Right. Good idea! I'll have Indian, then.

Pete and Jessica prepare to move again

A few poppadoms, do you think?
Pete (*furiously*) If you like!

Pete tries to get Jessica moving again, but she has thought of something

Jessica But, George—surely you won't need to pop out for poppadoms?
George Won't I?
Jessica Of course you won't! Sarah will cook you a meal when she gets back from her party.
Pete I thought you were anxious to go?
Jessica Yes—sorry! Of course I am, darling! (*She takes Pete's arm, happily*)
Pete Right! Off we go, then!

Pete and Jessica start to go once more

But at that moment Sarah and Margot come in from the garden and see Pete with a pretty lady on his arm. They stop and stare at them in surprise

Pete and George freeze in horror

Margot Just as I thought! He's entertaining loose women!

Pete hastily extricates himself from Jessica's clutches and escapes to George

Pete We're not loose women, are we, George?
George Certainly not! We're just good friends. (*He links arms with Pete, cosily*)

Pete reacts and escapes from George, thinking this is not helpful

Jessica looks at Margot and Sarah, and jumps to conclusions

Jessica Ah! You must be the neighbours!
Margot Neighbours?!
Jessica Pete said you might pop in. Let me introduce myself——
Pete There's no need for that!
Jessica (*surprised*) Pete…!
Pete You're not staying, so there's no point in making friends with the neighbours.
Margot *We* are not neighbours!
Jessica You mean you *don't* live nearby?
Margot Nearby? Never! (*To Sarah*) I knew if we took him by surprise we'd catch him in flagrante!
Jessica (*laughing*) Oh, I don't think we were that!
Pete No, certainly not!
Margot You were, arm-in-arm with this—this *woman*! (*She points an accusing finger at Jessica*)
Jessica (*happily*) Yes, of course he was! And shall I tell you why?
Pete She doesn't want to know why!
Margot Yes, she does!

George intervenes, helpfully

George She was just giving him a helping hand.
Margot Yes, I could see that!
George He—he tripped, you see? Over the edge of the carpet.
Pete Quite right, George! It's these new shoes. I haven't got used to them yet. If it hadn't been for Jessica grabbing my arm I might have ended up on the floor.
Jessica (*laughing*) Oh, Pete…!
Margot Is *that* her name? Jessica?
Pete Yes. I think so. (*He turns to Jessica*) You did say your name was Jessica, didn't you?

Jessica laughs even more

Margot (*to Sarah*) Worse than I thought! He didn't even know her name!

Jessica goes to them, trying to control her amusement

Jessica Look, you really must let me explain—(*now getting a closer look at Sarah*)—wait a minute! I've seen you before. Yes—of course! You're the girl in the picture over there! You're *Sarah*, aren't you?

Sarah and Margot axchange a look, rather surprised by Jessica's knowledge

Sarah Yes, I am! And this is my house!
Jessica I know. Pete told me all about you.
Sarah (*puzzled*) He *did*?
Jessica Of course!
Margot (*the voice of thunder*) And I am her mother!

Jessica looks at Pete, uncertainly

Pete Yes. She *is*…!
Jessica Oh, dear… (*To Margot, apologetically*) I'm *so* sorry.
Pete (*aside to George*) So am I, but it's too late to do anything about it now…!
Jessica You must have thought me so rude thinking that you were the neighbours. (*To Sarah*) I should have realized who you were straight away. (*She turns to look at George*) George—she's back!
George Sorry?
Jessica Sarah's back!

George looks in the direction of Sarah as if to confirm this

George Good lord, so she is! (*He gives a small wave*) Hallo, Sarah.
Sarah (*puzzled*) Hallo, George…
Jessica Well? Aren't you going to kiss her?

George considers this, briefly

George I hadn't thought of it…
Jessica Well, I think you *should*!
Pete Yes! *I* think you should too!
George I don't expect she wants me to…
Jessica Of course she does! Don't you, Sarah?
Sarah (*with a shrug*) I'm not bothered…

Jessica Doesn't he *always* kiss you when you come in?
Sarah Only if he's very drunk. (*She gives Margot a puzzled look*)
Jessica Well, *I* think you're very lucky to be married to such a nice man.
Pete Yes, so do I!
Margot "Nice men" don't entertain other women when their wives are out of the house! (*She glares at Jessica*)
Jessica Oh, I'm sure he doesn't do that!
Sarah Then what are *you* doing here?

Jessica laughs and crosses to Sarah

Jessica Oh, I think you're a bit confused, Sarah. I'm not here to meet your husband!
Sarah Then what *are* you here for?
Jessica (*noticing*) You poor girl! What *have* you done to your ankle?
Sarah I ... I sprained it.
Jessica Oh, dear. I *am* sorry. How did it happen?
Pete I wouldn't ask. It's a long story.
Jessica If you've sprained your ankle you should be sitting down and resting it. Shouldn't she, George?
Margot What has Sarah's ankle got to do with George?
Jessica Well, he may be reluctant to kiss her at the moment, but that doesn't mean that he no longer cares.
Pete No, of course it doesn't! You still care for Sarah, don't you? (*He gives George a sharp nudge*)
George (*enthusiastically*) Yes—rather! (*He grins, obediently*) I've always been fond of Sarah.

Sarah is rather surprised by George's bonhomie

Sarah You seem very cheerful tonight...
George Oh, good. I like to be cheerful. (*He smiles, cheerfully*)
Margot Why *shouldn't* George be cheerful?
Sarah I just didn't think he would be. Not *tonight*...
George Why ever not?
Sarah (*embarrassed*) Well—because of your ... your problem.
Margot I didn't know George had *got* a problem.
George (*quietly*) Neither did *I*...!
Sarah I know it was supposed to be a secret, but——
Pete (*glaring at her*) Do we have to talk about this *now*?
Jessica (*amused*) *You* don't seem very cheerful, and *you* haven't got a problem.
Margot Oh, yes, he has...!

George (*to Sarah*) Why on earth should you think that I'd got a problem?
Sarah Well ... wasn't that what you wanted to talk to Pete about?
George (*realizing*) Oh, that! No, no! That wasn't *my* problem!
Pete (*to Sarah*) There you are, you see! He doesn't have a problem, so there's no need to discuss it!
Jessica Well, he does have a *little* problem...
George (*outraged*) I do *not*!
Jessica Only he's far too polite to mention it. Poor George... (*She smiles at him, sympathetically*)
Margot Then you'd better tell us what it is!
Jessica He's simply longing for food, that's all! The poor man's starving!
Pete (*relieved*) Yes—exactly! Just look at him! He's lost half a stone since Saturday.

Sarah looks at George, trying to understand what the fuss was all about, and feeling a little disappointed

Sarah So ... was *that* all you were going to talk to Pete about? *Food*?!
George Well, no, not *just* food...
Pete Yes, it was! Food! That's all! Nothing else! Just food! (*He stares at George, desperately, hoping for back-up*) You are hungry, aren't you?
George Well ... yes. I am a bit peckish.
Jessica He was going to get himself a take-away because he thought that Sarah wasn't going to be here to cook a meal for him tonight.
Margot Why on earth should Sarah cook a meal for George?
Jessica Isn't that what usually happens? (*To Sarah*) You *do* cook for George, don't you?
Sarah (*bemused*) Well ... not *every* night, no... Occasionally, I suppose. On a Sunday. Or Christmas or something. But not ... on a regular basis.
Jessica (*rather puzzled by this*) Anyway, now you've sprained your ankle I don't suppose you'll feel up to cooking him an omelette or something, will you?
Sarah Well, I suppose I might just manage an omelette...
Margot My daughter has had a nasty fall. I don't see why she should be expected to cook meals for people who happen to be passing.
Jessica But George isn't just passing. Are you, George? (*She smiles, romantically*)
George I'm not quite sure... (*He looks at Pete, helplessly*)
Jessica (*to Sarah*) And I can't think why you went out when you had a sprained ankle.
Pete (*quietly*) I'm glad she did! (*He exchanges a look with George*)
Jessica I suppose you were going to the doctor to get it bandaged?

Margot She doesn't need a doctor! I am a trained surgeon and perfectly capable of bandaging my daughter's ankle.

Jessica Then I'm surprised you allowed her to go out with an injured foot. (*To Sarah*) Where did you have to go that was so important?

Sarah (*a little ashamed*) I ... I went to a party.

Jessica A party?! With a sprained ankle? Wasn't that rather dangerous?

George It certainly was! She went with her mother!

George and Pete enjoy this enormously. Margot glares at them

Jessica Ah! So *that* was what you were talking about? (*To Margot*) Before you and Sarah arrived these two were trying to decide how long a party of invalids and old ladies would last! (*She laughs*)

Margot *I* am not an old lady!

Sarah And *I* am not an invalid!

Margot Yes, you are! (*She gives Sarah a push to remind her*)

Sarah, now remembering, cries out in agony and clutches her ankle, dramatically. Jessica hastens to assist Sarah

Jessica You poor thing! You must be in such pain. You're a very brave girl. George! I really think you should give her a kiss.

George Do I *have* to?

Pete Yes, you do!

Pete pushes George firmly in the direction of Sarah. The momentum of the push carries him speedily to her, his arms outstretched, where he embraces her extravagantly. Margot watches this spectacle in astonishment. Having done his duty, George releases Sarah, leaving her a trifle embarrassed

Pete There you are, you see! That wasn't very difficult, was it? Now I shall kiss her mother! (*He sets off*)

Margot You will *not*! (*She turns away from him*)

Pete No. Perhaps you're right...

Margot now finds that she is facing the bottle of champagne. She picks it up and holds it aloft

Margot And what is *this*, may I ask?

Pete Sorry?

Margot You've been drinking champagne!

Pete Ah. Yes. We did have a glass.

Margot I thought champagne was only for special occasions. (*She glares at*

Jessica) Does this woman's presence here tonight denote that *this* is a special occasion?

Pete No! No—not at all!

Jessica (*disappointed*) Pete…! Of course it is!

Pete It was George's idea!

George Was it?

Pete You know very well it was! You got the bottle out of the fridge—and you opened it!

George Ah—yes. I did, didn't I…?

Sarah So what were you celebrating?

Pete Nothing!

Margot Celebrating nothing?

Pete Yes. But George said that we'd *make* it a special occasion by having champagne when it wasn't. So we did.

Jessica But Pete—today *is* a special occasion! A special occasion for *us*! (*Taking his arm, impulsively*) Come on, let's tell them all about it!

Margot (*to Sarah*) There! You see? I knew it! What did I tell you? I was right about him all along!

Whereupon, Sarah cries noisily. Jessica, surprised by such an emotional reaction from "George's wife", goes to Sarah sympathetically

Jessica Oh, Sarah dear—there's no need for you to cry. One day *you*'ll have a special occasion too. (*With a sudden happy thought*) Perhaps you'll have a *baby*! You and George must just try a little harder.

Which only makes Sarah cry even louder, and she runs from the room, forgetting her sprained ankle and omitting to limp

George notices this and gives it some thought

Margot (*to Jessica*) Now see what you've done! The sooner you two leave this house the better!

Jessica (*smiling, innocently*) That's what we were trying to do! If you hadn't arrived when you did we would have been elsewhere by now—making up for lost time.

Margot I might have guessed! From the very moment he and Sarah were married I knew there was something shifty about him. And now I know! I shall go and tend to my daughter's injured ankle. (*She starts to go*)

George If it *is* injured…

Margot What are you suggesting?

George Well, she went out of here like a gazelle.

Pete Yes, she did, didn't she? *I* noticed that. There was a definite touch of impala about her. (*He executes a small impala jump*)

Margot (*to Jessica*) I suggest you and your paramour go "elsewhere" and start sifting through your sordid memories!

Margot storms out

Jessica watches her go, unable to understand her vehement attitude. George chuckles to himself

Pete What's so funny?
George I never thought of you as a paramour!
Pete She wasn't talking about *me*, you fool!
George Wasn't she?
Pete (*glaring at him*) Of course she wasn't! *You*'re the one who's married to Sarah, not *me*!
George Ah—yes—of course. I forgot.

Jessica goes to Pete and links arms with him

Jessica Come on, then, darling! We'd better go while we've still got the chance.

Pete holds back

Pete Ah—yes—but … there is a bit of a snag, now…
Jessica I thought you and I were going to *your* house in Highgate Road to consummate our reunion.
Pete Yes—I know that was the idea—but *now* perhaps it would be better if you went with George.
Jessica With *George*?!
George With *me*?!
Pete For the time being. While I sort things out here.
Jessica But I don't want to go with George!
George Neither do I…!
Jessica Anyway, surely it's better for George to stay here and sort things out for himself?
Pete But you saw the state those two were in! Sarah and her mother are rather *off* George at the moment, so I couldn't leave him all alone here with them, could I? He'd be outnumbered.
Jessica But he *lives* here!
Pete Yes. I know he lives here. So he's had experience of what it's like here. He knows what Sarah and her mother are like when they're roused. Don't you, George?
George Yes, I do! Horrible!

Pete So I'd better stay here for a while and sort things out *for* him. You know—pour water on troubled oil.

George Isn't it usually the water that's troubled?

Pete Ah—yes. Absolutely.

Jessica But how long will that take?

Pete Oh—hard to tell. Isn't it, George?

George Yes...!

Pete These women are unpredictable. Aren't they, George?

George Yes...!

Pete It's a case of like mother like daughter. Isn't it, George?

George Yes!

Jessica sulks a little

Jessica Well, it's very disappointing...

Pete It's only a temporary set-back. You'll soon get over it. George can cook you an omelette. After all, he's had plenty of practice on all the occasions when Sarah wouldn't cook for him. You know where everything is in *my* house, don't you, George? Cooking oil. Eggs. Pepper. All that?

George (*giving him a stern look*) Yes. I think so...

Pete (*to Jessica*) And I'll be as quick as I can, I promise.

Jessica You'd better be! I'm looking forward to being alone with you again after all this time. (*She kisses him, enthusiastically*)

Pete is anxious to make it a brief embrace, and tries to escape from her clutches

Pete (*emerging*) No, Jessica——

Jessica pulls him back, abruptly, and continues the interrupted kiss. Pete struggles. George hastily intervenes and pulls them apart like a referee in a boxing match

George You haven't got time for all that!

Jessica There's no hurry, is there?

Pete Yes, there is! George's wife and her mother might come back!

Jessica Well, I wasn't kissing *George*!

George Anyway, Pete's got to find the oil to pour on the troubled water.

Jessica (*to Pete*) Well, don't keep me waiting too long or I'll come back and fetch you!

Pete No, no! You mustn't do that!

Jessica Come on, then, George!

Jessica goes out into the hall

George starts to follow her, then has a sudden thought and ambles back to Pete, thinking deeply

George I've just had a thought...
Pete This is no time for thoughts!
George When you've finished pouring oil on the troubled water *here* ... how are you going to explain to Sarah and her mother that you're now going off to my house to see Jessica?

Pete glances, nervously, towards the hall and closes to George

Pete Well, I'm *not*, am I?
George Aren't you?
Pete No. Not *now!*
George Oh. (*A beat*) Jessica thinks you are.
Pete So you'll have to explain to her, won't you?
George In the middle of cooking the omelette?
Pete Whenever you like!
George But I thought you said you were going to tell Jessica about Sarah and she was going to be understanding and go back to the Himalayas.
Pete That was before Sarah came back from her party! The situation's different now.
George So I'm going to be left on my own cooking an omelette for Jessica?
Pete (*trying to be patient*) George—I can't tell Jessica about Sarah before I tell Sarah about Jessica, can I?
George Why not? You were married to Jessica *first.*
Pete Yes. But I'm married to Sarah *now!*
George So what am I going to tell Jessica when you don't show up at my house to consummate your reunion?
Pete Well, I'll telephone you, won't I?
George How will that help? She's expecting more from you than a telephone call!
Pete You'll have to tell her that something important has cropped up.
George More important than a first wife coming back from the dead?
Pete Tell her I've had to go up to town urgently for a business appointment and that I'll meet her at your place tomorrow night instead.
George I see. Right. (*A beat*) You think she'll believe that?
Pete That's up to you, isn't it? That's what friends are for. You're good at making speeches. And that'll give me time to stay here and tell Sarah about Jessica.
George (*doubtfully*) With her *mother* still in the house?
Pete I'll get rid of the mother first!
George You will? I'd like to see that...

Pete George—*I* can handle Sarah's mother.
George Are you sure?
Jessica (*off*) George!

Jessica looks in from the hall

Are we going or not?
Pete He's just on his way! (*He pushes George towards her*)
Jessica See you soon, darling!
Pete Yes. Right...
Jessica (*pointing at him, playfully*) Half an hour—no more!

Jessica goes back into the hall

George You don't really think you're going to get away with this, do you?
Pete I might... Anyway, it was *you* who invited her here! So the least you
   can do is give her a bed for the night.
Jessica (*off*) George!
George Coming!

George races out into the hall

We hear the front door slam. Pete relaxes

Margot enters, talking as usual as she arrives

Margot Well, George? Have they gone? (*She sees Pete*) You're still here!
Pete (*calmly*) Of course I'm still here. I live here. Or had you forgotten?
Margot You're the one who has forgotten. Forgotten your own wife!
Pete No, I haven't! She misunderstood the situation. I'm just going to explain
   to her. (*He starts to go*)
Margot (*barring his way*) It's too late now for explanations! We assumed
   that you and your "lady-friend" would have had the decency to have gone
   by now.
Pete She's not my "lady-friend"!
Margot You expect me to believe that?
Pete No—but it happens to be true!
Margot You know what you've done to your wife, don't you?
Pete I haven't done anything to her. She tripped over the Hoover.
Margot She went out of here crying!
Pete I know! I heard her! (*He moves a little closer to her with a smile, anxious
   to ingratiate himself*) Look—er—Margot...

Margot eyes him, suspiciously

Margot *Now* what are you up to?

Pete (*glowing with gratitude*) I was just thinking how fortunate it was that you were able to come over here today and bandage Sarah's ankle for her.

Margot Oh, yes?

Pete I know she was very grateful. And so was I! (*Deeply impressed*) And you even took her to Isobel's party! *And* brought her back safely—which we both very much appreciated. (*He holds his grateful smile for a moment*) But—er…

Margot Yes. I thought there'd be a "but"!

Pete (*modestly*) Well, you see, Margot—*I'*m here now, aren't I? So *I* can look after Sarah. After all, we wouldn't want to impose on your good nature, would we? (*Generously*) So you don't need to hang around here any longer. You might just as well go back home. Don't you agree? (*He smiles at her, hopefully*)

Margot You don't think I'm going to leave my only daughter alone here with *you*?

Pete keeps smiling, trying to retain his equilibrium

Pete She *has* been alone with me before, Margot.

Margot Not under *these* circumstances! (*She glances around*) So where have you hidden her?

Pete I haven't hidden her anywhere! She's in the kitchen.

Margot Not Sarah! *Jessica!*

Pete (*thinking very hard*) Ah—now let's see—where have I hidden Jessica? I seem to have forgotten… (*Then he pretends to remember and chuckles at the thought*) Oh—yes—of course! I put her in the cupboard with the carpet sweeper! (*Losing his patience*) Of course I haven't hidden her!

Margot Then what *have* you done with her?

Pete Well, if you must know—she went off with George!

Margot With *George*?!

Pete Yes! To *his* house!

Margot Why on earth should she go to George's house?

Pete Ah… (*He hesitates, uncertain of his next move*)

Margot Well, come on! There must be a reason!

Pete There *is*! (*Aside*) When I can think of it…!

Margot Then tell me what it is!

And Pete proceeds to burn his boats

Pete You—you mean you didn't realize?

Margot Realize what?

Pete (*desperately*) Oh, for heaven's sake, Margot—Jessica is George's *wife*!

Margot looks astonished, and Pete sinks on to the sofa, realizing the situation into which he has now put himself

Black-out

END OF ACT I

ACT II

A few moments later

Pete is alone, still sitting on the sofa, deep in thought, muttering unintelligibly to himself as he contemplates confession. He decides to practise a little, and gets up

Pete Look, darling—there's something I forgot to tell you. (*He loses heart*) No—that's no good! (*He wanders a little, thinking hard*) Let's see now... (*With another idea*) Ah—yes—I've got it! (*He faces an imaginary Sarah*) Now, darling—er—perhaps you'd better sit down? (*He indicates the sofa and watches "her" as she crosses and sits down, then sits beside her*) You see—the thing is—you remember when we got married——

A door opens, and Sarah is standing there

Sarah Pete!

Pete jumps, nervously

Pete Aah! (*He turns and sees her*)
Sarah It's not *true*, is it?
Pete Sorry?
Sarah About George being married!
Pete Oh—that. (*He realizes it is now too late*) Yes...
Sarah Married to...?
Pete Jessica. Yes...
Sarah But I thought that *you*——
Pete I know what you thought!
Sarah How awful...! (*She hops towards him*)

Pete watches her approach with interest

Pete Why are you hopping?
Sarah I ... I twisted my ankle...
Pete Well, just now you ran out of here as if you were competing in the five hundred metres.

Sarah lowers her head, suitably ashamed. Pete smiles

Pete You *didn't* trip over the Hoover, did you?
Sarah (*shaking her head*) No… (*She runs the remaining distance and sits beside him, impulsively*) My mother says I should apologize.
Pete For hopping?
Sarah For suspecting you.
Pete She's a fine one to talk. You shouldn't listen to your mother.
Sarah Sorry…
Pete What?
Sarah I'm apologizing. (*She kisses his cheek*)
Pete Oh. Right. Thanks. (*A beat*) Is *she* going to apologize too?
Sarah I expect so.
Pete *She's* not going to kiss me as well, is she?
Sarah Why didn't he tell me?
Pete Who?
Sarah George! About being married.
Pete It probably slipped his mind.
Sarah But I was so rude to his wife!
Pete Not as rude as your mother was!
Sarah He never even mentioned it. You'd have thought it'd have been the first thing he'd say when he saw me.
Pete Oh, I … I expect he was embarrassed.
Sarah He's not ashamed of her, is he?
Pete I don't know. I'll have to ask him.
Sarah And why didn't *you* tell me? I am your wife, aren't I?
Pete Yes! Yes—of course you are!
Sarah (*pointing at him, playfully*) And you shouldn't have secrets from your wife.
Pete No! Of course not! Never! But, you see, I didn't know about it before. It … It's only just happened.

Sarah smiles, excitedly, her romantic nature coming to the fore

Sarah You mean they're newlyweds?
Pete Yes. I suppose they are…! Comparatively.
Sarah Good heavens! They're not on their honeymoon, are they? (*She giggles at the prospect*)
Pete Oh, no. This is no place for a honeymoon. I expect they did all that elsewhere.
Sarah Where's that?
Pete I'm not sure. Somewhere in the East, I think.
Sarah Where did it happen, then?

Pete What?
Sarah The consummation!
Pete Oh, I don't think he told me that.
Sarah (*realizing*) So *that* was why you'd all been drinking champagne? To celebrate George's wedding.

Pete is grateful for the suggestion

Pete Yes! Of course! Exactly! We were celebrating George's wedding! *You* can have a glass if you like. (*He gets up and goes to pour a glass of champagne*) You don't mind using the bridegroom's glass, do you? He's a very clean sort of person. (*He brings the glass of champagne to her*)
Sarah Oo, thanks! (*She raises her glass*) Well—here's to George and—er...
Pete Jessica. Yes—Jessica, I think.
Sarah George and Jessica! (*She sips her champagne*)

Pete suddenly loses heart, unable to keep up the pretence

Pete It's no good! I can't go through with this. You see, the thing is... Perhaps you'd better sit down?
Sarah I *am* sitting down.
Pete Ah—yes. So you are. (*So he sits beside her*) Darling—there's something I've got to tell you!

But before he can, Margot marches in

Margot I *told* her!
Pete What?
Margot About George being married.
Pete Oh, that. Yes. I know you did.
Margot (*noticing the champagne*) You seem to be drinking champagne!
Sarah Yes! And now we know why *they* had all been drinking champagne, don't we?
Margot Do we?
Pete Yes—exactly! (*He gets up*) Would *you* like a glass?
Margot No, thank you! This is very embarrassing after the way I spoke to his wife...
Sarah (*with a smile*) You'll have to apologize.
Margot Will I?
Sarah And not just to Jessica. To my husband, as well!
Margot Your husband?
Pete I'm over here!
Margot I never apologize to family. (*To Pete*) Why didn't you tell me about George's marriage just now when they were here?

Pete (*quietly*) I didn't *think* of it then…!

Margot What?!

Pete I didn't think it was a good time then! I knew George would want to tell you himself. After all, it is a personal matter. I didn't want to go blurting it out to all and sundry, did I?

Margot But you *did*!

Pete Did?

Margot Just now! You blurted it out to *me*!

Pete Yes, I did, didn't I? That was a bad mistake…

Margot So how long have you and George held this little secret between you?

Sarah Pete only heard about it tonight.

Margot Tonight?!

Pete Yes. I *told* Sarah he wanted to speak to me urgently about something. Well, that's what it was all about.

Margot To break the news of his nuptials?

Sarah Yes. That's why they opened the champagne!

Margot I see… (*She sits down, uncertain about this scenario*) But George and Jessica didn't appear to be in the early stages of married bliss… (*She ponders on this*)

Pete Well, I don't suppose they've got into the swing of it yet.

Sarah What was it you wanted to tell me, darling?

Pete Sorry?

Sarah Just now—before Mummy came in.

Pete Oh—er—it doesn't matter. I'll tell you later—after Mummy goes out.

Margot looks up from her reverie

Margot So how did it all come about?

Pete Sorry?

Margot This unexpected liaison between George and Jessica.

Pete Ah—well… (*He thinks hard*)

Sarah And why weren't you his best man? After all, he was yours.

Pete Yes. Yes, that's true. But, you see, I wasn't in Tibet at the time.

Margot and Sarah stare at him, both bewildered

Margot Tibet?! Who said anything about Tibet?

Pete Well, that's where it happened apparently.

Margot A marriage in Tibet? Perhaps I *will* have a glass of champagne…

Pete Yes—of course! (*He hastens away to pour it for her*) You can use the bride's glass.

Margot is not sure that this is acceptable to her, but manages to remain silent

Sarah What on earth was George doing in Tibet?

Pete That's a very good question...!

Margot And do *you* have a very good answer?

Pete Oh—er—he was there on business, I think.

Margot Then he should have kept his mind *on* his business, shouldn't he?

Pete Yes, I suppose so. (*Returning with a glass of champagne*) But you do meet people—especially in Tibet—and one thing leads to another. *You know how it is, Margot!*

Margot No, I do not! (*She accepts the glass and carefully wipes the rim for safety's sake*)

Sarah I never knew that George went to Tibet on business...

Pete Well, you know what he's like. Very modest. Doesn't talk much about himself.

Margot Secretive!

Pete Well, no. Margot—I wouldn't say secretive exactly. More ... reserved.

Sarah So he went to Tibet on business...

Pete Yes. And when he went there he was *single*——

Margot And when he came back he was *married*?

Pete Yes. *I* was surprised, too!

Margot (*severely*) Why?

Pete Sorry?

Margot Why were you surprised to hear that George was married? Do you know something about him that might render such an event unlikely?

Pete Oh, no—nothing like that!

Margot I'm very glad to hear it.

Pete Would you like a cheese biscuit? (*He darts away to fetch a tin of biscuits*)

Margot No, thank you. I'm far too intrigued to make any headway with food.

Pete No. Right.

Sarah I'd like a cheese biscuit.

Pete Oh, good! (*He hastens to her with the biscuits*) I'd hate it if there were no takers. There we are! All different shapes and sizes. Big ones, little ones. Thin ones, fat ones.

Sarah helps herself to a biscuit

I'll leave them here. Within easy reach. Then you can help yourself as often as you like.

Sarah (*laughing*) I do *live* here, Pete!

Pete Yes. Of course you do. I'm getting confused.

Margot So how—in Tibet—did George meet Jessica?

Pete Oh, I think you'd better ask *him* that.

Margot But *he* isn't here!

Pete No. That's true. But I'm sure he'd prefer——-
Margot Tell us what happened!
Pete Yes. Right. Well, you see—and you may find this hard to believe—she'd fallen off a mountain.
Sarah (*wide-eyed*) Fallen off a mountain?
Pete You see? I knew you'd find it hard to believe!
Margot She doesn't appear to have sustained any lasting injury.
Pete No. That's true. *I* noticed that. (*To Sarah*) Not even a sprained ankle!

Pete and Sarah laugh at this

Margot So George met her at the foot of the mountain? After she fell?
Pete Well… I'm not certain of the exact logistics of it…
Sarah We'll have to ask *her* about that.
Pete Ah—no! No, you mustn't do that!
Margot Why ever not?
Pete Well, it's a matter of pride, I suppose. If you're a mountain climber you don't like to fall off, do you? It's like a jockey falling off a horse. So, whatever happens, don't mention it to her!
Margot That'll be very difficult.
Sarah (*romantically*) Was it love at first sight?

Pete turns to look at her, having lost the plot for a minute

Pete Sorry?
Sarah When they met.
Pete Oh. I'm not sure about that. It may have been. Anything can happen in Tibet.
Sarah *I* think it sounds *very* romantic… (*She sighs, romantically*)
Pete Do you? Oh, good. So do I. (*He also sighs, romantically*)
Margot Will they be coming back tonight?
Pete I hope not…!
Margot What?
Pete Well, they probably never had a honeymoon in Tibet. So I expect they'll be making up for lost time in Highgate Road.
Sarah What a pity! I'm longing to say congratulations to George.
Pete No, you mustn't do that!
Sarah Why ever not?
Pete I think they probably want to keep it a secret.
Margot Keep their marriage a secret?
Pete Yes.
Margot Why?
Pete *Why?*

Margot There must be a reason!
Pete Yes, there *is*…!
Margot So what is it?
Pete I … I don't think he's told his parents yet.
Margot His parents?! They must be quite elderly. Are they likely to raise objections?
Pete Well, some people don't approve of ladies climbing mountains.

And at that moment George and Jessica walk in from the garden

Pete reacts with alarm and goes to them, urgently

You're not supposed to be here! You're supposed to be in Highgate Road!
George We were. But we couldn't get in.
Pete Why not?
George Because *you*'ve got the key!
Pete What? (*Then he remembers*) Oh, my God—so I have! (*He hastily takes George's key out of his pocket and hands it to him*) There you are, then! Off you go! Don't hang about here! (*He tries to urge George and Jessica back towards the garden*)
Sarah *Hallo*, George…!

They look back and see Sarah and Margot, side-by-side, smiling with delight. Sarah waves to George, secretively

George (*puzzled*) Hallo, Sarah…
Sarah *Hallo*, Jessica…! (*She waves to* her *in the same way*)

Jessica is surprised by Sarah's unexpected volte-face

Jessica Hallo, Sarah…
George (*aside, to Pete*) You haven't told her, have you?
Pete (*aside, to George*) I didn't get the chance!
Sarah (*playfully*) We didn't expect to see you two again tonight! Did we, Pete?
Pete No, we certainly didn't…!
Margot *Jessica*! (*She approaches Jessica, heavy with shame*) How can you forgive me?
Jessica Sorry?
Margot For the things I said! The accusations I made. I had no right to cast aspersions on your good character.
Jessica (*taken aback*) Oh. Well, that's very kind of you, Mrs—er… (*She hesitates, uncertainly*)

Margot (*with enormous generosity*) Margot! Call me Margot!

Jessica Well, thank you ... Margot. Of course I forgive you. It was an easy mistake to make.

Margot Nevertheless, I should never have said such things about you and— (*not wanting to break a confidence*)—and such a good, blameless gentleman.

Jessica You hear that, Pete?

Pete Yes—I certainly did! Did *you* hear that, George?

George What?

Pete Do pay attention! Margot's dishing out compliments.

George Oh—right!

Sarah (*impulsively*) It's no good, George, I've just *got* to kiss you! (*She rushes across to him*)

George looks at her in surprise

George Any particular reason?

Sarah (*with a big smile*) Yes! *Very* particular...!

Pete You don't have to kiss him if you don't want to! After all, he wouldn't kiss *you* at first, would he?

Sarah But I must! (*She kisses George enthusiastically*) I'm *so* pleased! (*She smiles at him happily*)

George Oh. Good. I'm glad you enjoyed it. (*He gives Pete a puzzled look*)

Jessica It's so nice to see a happy couple, isn't it, Margot? (*She gazes at Sarah and George*)

Margot Well, they're not exactly a *couple*, are they?

Jessica Aren't they? I thought they——

Margot Not a *real* couple—like *some* people—eh, Jessica? (*She smiles, knowingly*)

Jessica smiles, thinking Pete must have told them about her and Pete being married

Jessica Oh, good! I'm glad you approve. (*She joins Pete*)

Margot We certainly do! That's why we're drinking champagne.

Sarah Yes! We wanted—to show how happy we are for you!

Margot Absolutely!

Margot and Sarah go into a happy huddle and giggle together

Jessica (*quietly; to Pete*) Well! You *did* pour oil on the troubled water, didn't you?

Pete I'm not sure...!

Sarah (*reappearing out of the huddle*) But, Pete...?

Pete (*aside, to Jessica*) Here it comes…!
Sarah What were *you* doing with George's key?

Pete holds her look, blankly, for a moment

Pete Sorry?
Sarah He said just now that you'd got his key.
Pete D-did he?
Margot Yes! That's why he couldn't get into the house.
Jessica No, no, that wasn't George's key, that was *Pete's* key. He'd just forgotten to give it to George before we left. (*She giggles*)
Sarah But why should he give his key to George?
Jessica (*a little embarrassed*) Well—er—because he had things to see to *here*. Didn't you, Pete? (*She grins at Pete*)
Pete Yes, I certainly did…!
Margot (*enjoying the secret*) And *you* have things to see to in Highgate Road, don't you, Jessica?
Jessica Well, I hope so! (*She laughs*) We were going to celebrate something special…
Margot Yes! Of course you were! Weren't they, Sarah?
Sarah They certainly were!

Sarah and Margot return to their huddle and giggle together. Pete turns to George, anxiously

Pete You'd better go back to Highgate Road!
George Good idea! (*He prepares to go*)
Jessica No, George!

George stops

(*Whispering to Pete*) He doesn't need to go—not now you've poured oil on the troubled water! (*She laughs*)

Margot and Sarah come smiling out of their huddle

Margot George…
George (*aside to Pete*) Now what?
Margot You never told us that you'd been to Tibet.

George looks at her, blankly. Pete shifts, uncomfortably

George Tibet?

Margot (*playfully*) Don't say you've forgotten!

Margot and Sarah enjoy the joke

George I'm not sure... (*To Pete*) Have I been to Tibet?
Pete Of course you have! (*He nods, desperately*)
Jessica Good heavens! What a coincidence!
Margot Don't pretend you didn't know, Jessica!

Margot and Sarah laugh together

Jessica I certainly didn't know that *George* had been there.
George Neither did I...! I don't even know where it is...
Pete Of course you know where it is!
Sarah There's no need to be shy, George. We know all about it.
George All about me going to Tibet?
Sarah Yes! I'm sorry—I know it was meant to be a secret...
George It *is*! It's a secret from *me*!
Pete (*desperately*) But you told me all about it!
George Did I?
Pete Of course you did!
George I must have forgotten...
Jessica Did Sarah go with you?
George (*amused at the prospect*) Sarah? No. I don't think so. I'm sure I'd
   have remembered that.
Margot Why on earth should Sarah want to go with George? She'd far rather
   go with Pete.

Which, naturally, comes as a surprise to Jessica

Jessica Would she?
Margot Of course!
Pete No, she wouldn't! She'd prefer to go with George any day!
Sarah Pete...!
Jessica That's what I thought!
George But what was I doing in Tibet?
Margot Being a naughty boy by all accounts!

Margot and Sarah enjoy the joke

Pete Come on, George! Surely you remember?
George No! I don't!

Pete glares at him

Sarah But that's where it all happened! (*Romantically*) You must remember *that*, George...

George I don't remember *being* there, never mind what happened...

Pete Yes, you do!

George (*all at sea*) No, no! Now *you*'re getting confused. It was Jessica who was in Tibet. She told *me* all about it. Didn't you, Jessica? On the phone. On your return.

Jessica Yes, I did.

George And I told Pete.

Pete (*glaring at him*) Yes, you *did*...!

Sarah But you were in Tibet, too, George. That's where you and Jessica first met.

Jessica No, no! We met in *this* country. Long before I went to Tibet. And it was a very special occasion. Surely you remember *that*, George?

Pete No, he doesn't!

Jessica Well, I do... (*With a big smile*) And so do you, don't you, Pete?

Sarah (*disappointed*) So it wasn't love at first sight, then?

Jessica Sorry?

Sarah When you first met George.

Jessica (*amused at the thought*) Well ... no. Not exactly. I mean, I'm very fond of him, of course, but our friendship hasn't developed into a grand passion. Has it, George?

George I'm not quite sure...

Margot If your friendship hasn't developed into a grand passion I'm surprised you have allowed your relationship to proceed as far as it has.

Jessica I didn't think it *had* proceeded very noticeably.

Sarah Oh, you don't have to pretend! I know it was meant to be a secret, but Pete told us all about it.

George looks at Pete, horrified

George (*aside*) You *didn't*?!

Pete (*aside, nodding miserably*) I *did*...!

Sarah And we're delighted!

Jessica But what exactly *did* Pete tell you?

Sarah Well ... that you were in Tibet...

Jessica *And*?

Sarah And so was George...! (*She smiles at George, romantically*)

Pete Of course he was! Go on! Tell them all about it! (*He pushes George towards them, desperately, nodding encouragement*)

Now at last realizing what is expected of him, George suddenly becomes voluble on the subject, forcing himself to smile happily at the memory

George Yes! Yes, of course I was! I remember it all very clearly now—as if it was yesterday! I went to Tibet—and I found it a fascinating country! And it was there that I met Jessica! (*He points to Jessica, proudly*)

Jessica What?! (*She laughs*)

George She'd just fallen off a mountain! It was a pathetic sight. She was just lying there in the snow in her boots. All spikes and things. And a bobble hat!

Jessica (*laughing even more*) Oh, George...!

Sarah (*romantic again*) So it was love at first——-

Jessica *No*, Sarah!

George subsides into a chair, exhausted by his efforts, and glares at Pete

Margot You appear to have recovered from your fall very well. Were there no bones broken?

Jessica No. I was very lucky.

Margot You *must* have been...!

Jessica (*laughing*) I can't think why you're making all this up, George! Bobble hat indeed!

Sarah You mean it's not true?

Jessica Of course it's not! I certainly don't remember meeting George in Tibet.

Pete But you did lose your memory for a while.

Margot Did she?

Pete So you could well have forgotten the meeting.

Jessica Oh, I think I'd have remembered meeting George on the top of a mountain!

Sarah (*disappointed again*) So nothing happened between you?

Jessica Certainly not!

Pete Would anyone like a cheese biscuit?

All No!

Sarah But we thought that was where it all took place! It's what we've been celebrating—with champagne!

Margot Yes. And I've been using the bride's glass!

Jessica The *bride*?!

Sarah Yes. Pete said you'd gone to consummate your marriage in Highgate Road...

George (*aside, to Pete*) You *didn't*?!

Pete (*aside, to George*) I *did*...!

Jessica Our *marriage*? Whose marriage?

Sarah Yours and George's, of course!

Jessica stares at her for a moment in disbelief

Jessica George and I are not married!
Sarah You ... you aren't?
Jessica No! Of course not!
George (*aside, to Pete*) The waters are getting troubled again...!

Margot turns to face Pete, imperiously, about to explode

Margot How could you tell us such a cock-and-bull story?
Pete Oh, I don't think it was that! You must have misunderstood. (*He turns to point at George*) It's all *his* fault!
George Yes, I thought it would be...!
Pete He can be so confusing at times.
Jessica I'm surprised you thought I could do such a thing. Marry George indeed!
George It might not have been as bad as all that...
Jessica Oh, sorry, George! I didn't mean it that way. It's just that I wouldn't dream of trying to steal somebody else's husband.
Margot Somebody else's husband?
Jessica Yes! How could you think that I could do a thing like that to Sarah?
Margot To *Sarah*?
Sarah To *me*?
Jessica Yes!
Sarah But I'm not married to George!

Jessica holds her look for a moment, trying to digest this bit of information

Jessica Are you *sure*?
Sarah (*laughing*) I think I'd have remembered!
Jessica Then who *is* he married to?
George (*sadly*) I'm not married to *any*one...

Margot turns to Pete, who is still. And silent

Margot You're very quiet!
Pete I think it's just the calm before the storm...

Jessica closes in on Pete from the other side

Jessica Pete...!
Pete Y-yes?
Jessica You told me that Sarah was married to George!
Pete D-did I?
Jessica Yes, you did!

Pete Surely not? You must have misheard. Coming off the plane like that you were probably a bit jet-lagged.

Jessica I came by car and I remember it distinctly.

Sarah (*to Jessica*) I can't think why he told you that. I couldn't possibly be married to George.

Jessica Why not?

Sarah Because *I'm* married to *Pete*!

A dreadful moment

Jessica looks at Pete with a smile that could slice bacon. Pete cringes

Jessica Well! What a *lovely* surprise! (*With overdone enthusiasm*) Congratulations, Pete! You couldn't have chosen a nicer wife. Could he, George?

Which puts poor George in a bit of a spot regarding his loyalty

George Well... I—I'm not sure about that...

Sarah (*offended*) George!

George I don't mean you're *not* a nice wife! I'm sure you're very nice indeed. But I suppose there could be ... other women who might have made Pete a nice wife. I mean, you can't rule it out, can you? That's all I'm saying.

Jessica Let's ask him, then! Well, Pete? *Can* you imagine being married to anyone except Sarah?

Pete shifts uneasily

Sarah (*giggling*) You mustn't ask him that! I'm sure he had lots of possible wives before he married *me*.

Jessica (*quietly*) Yes, I *bet* he did...!

Margot Well, when he asked *my* daughter to marry him I hope he didn't have any other possible wives on his mind. (*She glares at Pete*)

Pete Look—do we have to talk about this?

Jessica Why not? After all, *some* men spend a lot of time picking over the possibles before getting married. Even making second or third choices. (*She smiles at Pete, innocently*)

Pete gives her a look

Margot I trust that Sarah was not a second or third choice?

Pete No—of course she wasn't!

Jessica (*quietly*) Not *third*, anyway...! (*She enjoys Pete's discomfort*)

Sarah Well—if it was a "special occasion" when George met Jessica—maybe it *was* love at first sight. They may not be married *now*—but they *could* be married in the future! And then Pete could be *George's* best man!

Jessica (*totally bewildered*) What *are* you talking about?

Margot (*to George*) Is that a likely scenario?

George Oh, I don't think I could tell you that…

Sarah (*smiling, hopefully*) Well, can you at least tell us if it was as special an occasion for you as it was for Jessica?

George I—I'm not sure…

Sarah Not sure?!

George It's a long time ago. I can't remember.

Jessica Well, *I* can remember it perfectly! It was a very very happy, very very special occasion for me. I remember the day so well—the sun was shining—the birds were singing——

Pete You don't have to go into details!

Sarah (*delightedly*) So at least we know that there's still hope! Come along, Mummy! Now we can see to the sandwiches.

Sarah runs off, happily, into the kitchen

Margot gives the others a doubtful look, and follows Sarah

Pete is left alone with Jessica. And George, of course. Jessica moves towards Pete. He cowers a little

Jessica Oh, Pete…! Why didn't you *tell* me that you'd got married again?

Pete It … it didn't seem to fit into the conversation.

Jessica It must have been an awful shock when George told you that I was here.

Pete Yes. It was a bit…

Jessica No wonder you pretended that Sarah was married to George. (*To George*) And why didn't *you* tell me that Pete had married again when I spoke to you on the phone? When I got here you gave that lovely welcoming speech—*and* poured champagne! I began to think that you were both pleased to see me. (*She looks suitably disappointed*)

George We were! Weren't we, Pete?

Pete Er—yes! Yes—of course we were pleased to see you!

Jessica Oh, good! Well, that's *some*thing! I assume you haven't told *Sarah* about *me*, either?

George No, he hasn't! (*He glares at Pete*)

Pete No. I haven't… (*He sits on the sofa in despair*)

Jessica Why ever not?

Pete Well, it … It didn't seem necessary.

Jessica Not necessary to tell your wife that you were already married?
Pete Well, when I married Sarah, I ... I didn't know that you were still alive.

Jessica looks at him with a glimmer of hope

Jessica You mean that would have made a difference?

Pete looks up, surprised that she needed to ask

Pete Of course it would have made a difference!

Jessica sits beside him, happily encouraged

Jessica Oh, Pete! That's the nicest thing you've said to me since I arrived. (*She kisses him on the cheek*)
Pete (*unhappily*) Oh, God...!
Jessica It's too late now for prayers.
Pete (*in quiet despair*) What the hell are we going to do about it?
George (*looking up, helpfully*) Whisky?
Pete Good idea!

George hastens away to pour three whiskies. Jessica looks at Pete, sympathetically

Jessica Poor Pete...! What a problem.
Pete Yes... Now I shall *have* to tell Sarah...
Jessica I meant *after* you've told Sarah. *That* problem.

Pete looks at her, briefly

Pete Ah. Yes...

George arrives with the drinks

George Whisky, Jessica?
Jessica (*taking it*) Thank you, George.
George Whisky, Pete?
Pete (*taking it*) Thank you, George.
George Whisky, George? Thank you, George. (*He raises his glass*) Well—er—perhaps I could?
Pete (*firmly*) *No*, George!
George No. Right. (*He sits nearby*)

They drink, independently. A moment's silence. All thinking

Jessica You didn't hang about, though, did you, darling? No sooner was I cold in my grave than you were out looking for a replacement.

Pete You weren't *in* your grave, though, were you?

Jessica No. But *you* didn't know that!

Pete We — we assumed.

Jessica Then you shouldn't have done! (*She starts to laugh*)

Pete What's so funny?

Jessica I might have turned up at your second wedding! You know—in that dreadful silence when they ask if anyone knows any just cause and all that. I might have stood up at the back and shouted "Yes—he's my husband".

Pete I'm glad you didn't...!

Jessica sips her whisky, thinking about it

Jessica So how long did you give me, then?

Pete Sorry?

Jessica Before you wrote me off and went in search of pastures new.

Pete We didn't "write you off"!

George No! We did make enquiries concerning your whereabouts.

Jessica Oh, good! Thank you, George. That is a relief. I'm glad you made enquiries.

Pete Well, of course we did! We didn't assume you were dead just because we hadn't had a card for a fortnight!

George No. We went out there and tried to find you.

Jessica (*appalled*) You *didn't*?!

Pete Of course we did!

Jessica To the Himalayas?

Pete Well, where *else* would we go to look for you?

Jessica (*avoiding his eyes*) Yes—of course...

George We checked your hotel and they said you'd left earlier than expected.

Pete So we advertised in the newspapers. Checked all the hospitals. But there was no sign of you anywhere.

Jessica So you were probably right, then. I—I *must* have fallen off a mountain...

George But where did you go to *after* you fell off a mountain?

Jessica (*helplessly*) I don't know, George. I just can't remember... So when you couldn't find me—you came back home?

Pete (*sadly*) There was nothing else we *could* do. We came back and waited. And hoped. But ... well ... after six months with no word—we — we did begin to lose heart. Didn't we, George?

George (*quietly, his head down*) We certainly did...

Pete And as time went on we realized that—that we weren't going to see you again ... and that we'd have to come to terms with it...

Jessica is very moved, her eyes watery

Jessica Oh. Pete...!

Jessica embraces Pete, and they hold on hard for a moment, then she turns to include George

Oh, George...!

George puts down his glass and goes quickly to sit beside her so she can embrace him also. They all cling on. Suffering. Meaning it

Then Margot walks in and sees them sitting in a row on the sofa

Margot Hear no evil, see no evil, speak no evil...!

Pete and George leap up and move away a little

I suppose this is what is known in the suburbs as a "love-in"?
Pete A "love-in"?
Margot A married man and a bachelor squashed on a sofa with a spinster.
Jessica I'm not a spinster!
Margot Yes, you are! You're unmarried, aren't you?
Pete Of course she is!

Jessica glares at him

Margot So that makes you a spinster!
Jessica (*rising, angrily*) Oh, no, it doesn't! As a matter of fact ——
Pete The embracing was all George's fault! (*To George, desperately*) Wasn't it?
George Certainly was! You see, I do tend to get overexcited sometimes when I look at Jessica.
Jessica Thank you, George!
George And when I do I'm afraid I get a bit——-
Pete Yes, all right! We don't want to hear the grisly details!
Margot (*coldly*) The sandwiches are ready—if you can get your mind off sex and on to sustenance!

Margot goes out again

Pete (*to Jessica*) You weren't going to *tell* her, were you?
George Well, she's going to have to be told *some* time!

Jessica Yes. I'm getting a very bad reputation.

Pete It's not going to be easy…

Jessica You should have thought of that before you committed bigamy.

Pete Is that what I've done?

Jessica Well, you married a second person when you were already married to a first person.

Pete But I didn't think the first person was still alive!

Jessica Well, she is! So you'll have to tell Sarah that she's no longer your wife and that I am.

Pete I can't do that! We've only been married six months.

Jessica (*as to a child*) Darling—you can only have one wife at a time. Not one man, *two* wives. One man, *one* wife.

George So you'll have to decide which one you want.

Jessica It's not a matter of choice, George.

George Isn't it?

Jessica No. He'll have to tell Sarah that I'm his first wife and that first wives take precedence over any subsequent wives. It's only fair. First things first.

Pete I couldn't do that! Sarah'll kill me!

George And if *she* doesn't, her *mother* will…!

Pete Anyway, I love Sarah. I'm not going to leave her just because you suddenly come back from the grave.

Jessica But I'm still married to you, darling.

Pete So is she! Anyway, I thought you said that you wouldn't dream of stealing somebody else's husband?

Jessica But I won't be stealing you. You were my husband first. I'll simply be taking what's mine by right.

Pete What right?

Jessica (*with a big smile*) First come, first served!

George tries to urge Pete on his way

George Come on, Pete! *This* time you've *got* to tell her.

Pete (*reluctantly*) Oh, all right. (*He hesitates, nervously*) But food first, eh?

George All right. Food first. (*Firmly*) But then it's confession time!

George goes out to the kitchen

Pete and Jessica face each other, a little sadly

Pete I … I'm very sorry.

Jessica So am I!

A beat

Pete You coming?

Jessica In a minute. I just want to powder my nose. I wouldn't want Sarah to think I'd been crying.

Pete No, neither would I…! (*He smiles, and is about to go, but hesitates*) I—er—I *am* glad to see you again, you know.

They hold their look for a moment, then Pete goes out to the kitchen

Jessica smiles, quite moved, takes out her compact and starts to powder her nose

Alan looks in from the garden. He is a good-looking man with a casual, relaxed manner. At first he does not see Jessica

Alan Hallo… Jessica…

Jessica turns and sees him. And he sees her. Jessica cannot believe her eyes

Jessica Alan! What the hell are *you* doing here?

Alan Looking for you, of course!

Jessica (*coldly*) I can't think *why*…

Alan Because you left me behind—in France! I came home this morning and you were driving off with your bags packed.

Jessica (*outraged*) You mean you followed me?

Alan Of course I followed you!

Jessica All the way from France?

Alan Yes!

Jessica (*a little put out*) You didn't catch me up, though, did you?

Alan (*amused*) Not likely! I wanted to find out where you were going!

Jessica Well, now you *know* because you saw me come in.

Alan Yes. And I've been sitting out there in my car waiting for you to come *out* again!

Jessica Why didn't you ring the bell if you were so keen to find me?

Alan Because there were … *people* inside. Moving about. Talking. I wasn't sure if I'd be welcome.

Jessica Well, you're not! (*Then, anxiously*) Did you … *see* anyone outside? While you were waiting.

Alan Oh, yes! I saw an old lady arriving with a young lady who appeared to be limping. (*He cannot understand why*)

Jessica But you didn't see anyone *else* — *leaving*? And then coming back again?

Alan No. I don't think so… (*He tries to remember*)

Jessica (*aside*) Thank God for that …!

Alan Mind you, I did nod off for a while.

Jessica Nod Off?! I thought you were eager to see me!

Alan Yes, I was. I *am*! But I was a bit tired, too. It's a hell of a long drive from France.
Jessica (*furiously*) Yes — I know! *I* did it, too!

Alan goes to her with a confident smile

Alan Anyway. I've found you! That's the main thing, isn't it? (*He embraces her*)
Jessica (*escaping from him*) Well, now you *have* found me you can go back to France again!
Alan Oh, good! You're coming with me, then? (*He takes her arm and tries to go*)
Jessica (*escaping again*) No! I am not!
Alan I thought we were happy together?
Jessica We were. Until you went off with another woman!
Alan (*with a shrug*) That's what happens in France. It wasn't serious. And I *was* on my way back to you this morning.
Jessica Well, you were too late!
Alan (*defensively*) I did ask you to marry me—remember?
Jessica (*avoiding his eyes*) Yes. Yes, I know you did…
Alan Three times! *Four* times, probably.
Jessica You were pissed the fourth time.
Alan Yes, but I still meant it. And you said no *every* time!
Jessica (*quietly*) I had a very good reason…! Anyway, that was no excuse for you to go off with other women!
Alan *One* other woman!
Jessica Anyway, I'm *here* now—and this is where I'm staying!
Alan (*puzzled*) Whose house *is* this, anyway?
Jessica It … it belongs to a friend of mine. Look, you can't stay here! There are people about—and they mustn't see you! You really must go!

Sarah comes in, carrying a plate of sandwiches

Sarah You're taking a long time to… (*She stops, seeing Alan*) Oh.
Alan Ah! You're the girl I saw outside! (*To Jessica*) *She*'s the girl I told you about.
Jessica Yes—I know!
Alan Doesn't seem to be limping anymore though. (*To Sarah*) Very nice house you've got.
Sarah Oh. Thanks. (*She smiles, shyly*)
Alan (*to Jessica*) Aren't you going to introduce us?
Jessica (*reluctantly*) This is Sarah. A very dear old friend of mine.

Sarah is a little surprised by this description of her

Alan Hallo, Sarah!

Alan and Sarah shake hands. Alan looks at Jessica, anticipating an introduction, but not getting one, he turns to Sarah again

I've got a name, too!

Sarah (*amused*) Oh, good!

Alan looks again at Jessica, but she still shows no sign of introducing him, so he looks at Sarah again

Alan It's Alan. That's *my* name—Alan! (*To Jessica*) Isn't it?

Jessica Well, that's what you *told* me!

Sarah (*puzzled by this*) Nice to meet you, Alan. Would you like a sandwich? (*She holds out the plate of sandwiches*)

Alan I certainly would. I'm starving! (*He takes one*) I've had a long journey, you see. (*He starts to eat*)

Sarah (*intrigued*) You haven't come from Tibet, by any chance?

Alan Oh, no! Not Tibet. Well, not Tibet *today*. Today I've come from France. So I am glad of a sandwich.

Sarah Perhaps you'd like a glass of wine to go with it?

Alan Well, that would be——

Jessica He doesn't want any wine!

Sarah Yes, he does. (*To Alan*) I'll get Pete to bring you some.

Alan Pete?

Sarah My husband.

Jessica You don't have to do that!

Sarah (*surprised by her vehemence*) Sorry?

Jessica He mustn't drink when he's driving. And he's driving *now*!

Alan Is he?

Jessica (*glaring at him*) Yes, he is!

Alan Oh, good! You're ready to go, then? (*He makes a move, hopefully*)

Jessica Not *me*! I'm not going anywhere!

Alan In that case I'm not in a hurry.

Sarah Perhaps you'd like another sandwich, then?

Jessica No, he wouldn't!

Alan Yes, he would. Thank you, Sarah. They're very nice. (*He takes another sandwich*) Is it all right if I sit down while I'm waiting for Pete to bring the wine?

Sarah Yes, of course.

Alan Thanks. (*He sits down*) Red, if there's a choice.

Sarah (*uncertain who he is*) Were you looking for someone? Or just passing?

Alan Oh, I was looking for someone all right! (*He grins at Jessica*)

Jessica Yes! He was looking for George!

Alan }
Sarah } (*together*) George?!

Jessica (*to Alan, trying to keep him quiet*) That *was* what you said when you came in, wasn't it?

Alan Was it?

Jessica Yes! You said, "Sorry to bother you, but I'm looking for George."

Alan (*bemused*) Did I say that?

Jessica Yes! You did! (*She nods, encouragingly*)

Alan (*thinking hard*) I didn't think I knew a George... You sure I didn't say Gerald? Or Arthur? Or Ramsey? I know quite a few Ramseys, strangely enough...

Jessica It was George! He's an old friend of yours! Surely you remember?

Alan Oh—*George*! I didn't realize you meant George. You should have said it as we do in France—(*assuming a heavy French accent*) "Georges! Georges!"—then I'd have known.

Sarah So he *is* a friend of yours?

Alan Apparently...

Sarah What a coincidence!

Alan May I have another sandwich?

Sarah Yes, of course!

Alan takes another sandwich

Jessica He hasn't got time for another sandwich! He's just going!

Sarah He can't go without seeing George. I'll go and fetch him.

Jessica You don't have to do that!

Sarah But Alan has come all the way from France to see his old friend George, so we'd better tell George that he's here. (*She turns to Alan with a knowing smile*) I bet I know what *this* is all about...!

Jessica (*aside*) I hope you don't...!

Sarah George has told you all about it, hasn't he?

Alan, sandwich poised, looks back at her, puzzled

Alan Has he?

Sarah (*delightedly*) You're going to be his best man, aren't you?

Alan, intent on his sandwich, stares at her blankly, trying to concentrate

Alan Whose best man?

Sarah *George*'s, of course!

Alan Is my old friend George getting married, then?

Sarah Didn't he tell you?

Alan (*trying to recall*) No. I don't think he mentioned it...

Sarah I can't think why he's keeping it a secret from *you* of all people.

Alan So who's he getting married to?

Jessica Don't be silly, Sarah! She's exaggerating. George isn't getting married to *anyone*! (*She gives Sarah a stern look*)

Sarah Well—no, I suppose it's not absolutely *definite*—but we're all hoping that's it's true. (*She smiles, optimistically*)

Alan Oh, great! And who's the lucky lady?

Sarah (*indicating Jessica, cheerfully*) Jessica, of course!

Which naturally comes as a surprise to Alan, and he hesitates for a moment before seeking clarification

Alan *This* Jessica?

Sarah Yes!

Jessica Don't take any notice of her!

Alan (*to Jessica*) You never told me you were going to marry my old friend George. No wonder you didn't want to go back to France!

Sarah (*gazing at Jessica, deeply impressed*) Don't tell me you've been to France as *well* as Tibet?

Alan Oh. She told you all about Tibet, then?

Sarah Well, I am a dear old friend of hers, aren't I? (*She looks at Jessica with a smile*)

Pete and George come in

Pete Are you two going to stay in here all night? (*He stops, seeing a third party*) Oh, I didn't know we had company.

Sarah (*impressively*) He's just arrived from France!

Pete He hasn't, has he? Good lord. (*To Alan*) Are you one of those men selling onions? Oh, no. You'd have had them hanging around your neck, wouldn't you?

George Come on, then, Sarah! Aren't you going to introduce us to your friend from France?

Jessica Don't be silly, *you* don't need an introduction!

George (*puzzled*) Don't I?

Jessica Although it must be a *bit* of a surprise for you. After all, you didn't know he was coming, did you?

George (*thinking hard*) No. No, I don't think I did. (*To Pete*) We didn't know he was coming, did we?

Pete Not that I remember... (*He tries to remember*)

Jessica Alan! Look who's here! It's your old friend *George*! (*She points, dramatically, at George*)

Alan looks across at George, severely, for a moment

Alan Good lord, so it is! (*He goes to George with an icy smile*) Well, well! It's good to see you again, "old friend"! (*He crushes George to him, abruptly, in a bear-like hug*)

George is rather surprised by the severity of this greeting and is relieved to escape from it

Pete (*to George*) You didn't tell me you had an old friend in France.
George No. He must have moved there recently.
Alan Eighteen months ago!
George As long as that? I'd never have guessed.
Alan (*glaring at him*) But now I'm *here*! And making my presence felt.
George Yes. I know you are…! (*He rubs his painful shoulder*)

Alan turns to look at Pete

Alan And I take it you must be Pete?
Pete Ah—yes. Yes, I think so. *I* don't know you as *well*, do I? (*He cowers a little for fear of a similar embrace*)
Alan (*uncertainly*) Er—I'm not sure… (*He turns to Jessica for guidance*) Do I know him as well?
Jessica No…!
Alan Right. (*To Pete*) No.
Pete Oh, good…
Alan But I know your wife!
Pete (*nervously*) Do you?
Alan And she's very nice.
Pete Is she? Oh, good.
Alan Surely you haven't forgotten your own wife? (*He laughs*)
Pete Oh, no—no, of course not!
Jessica It's just that sometimes he gets a little confused. (*She gives Pete a severe look*)
Alan (*indicating Sarah, playfully*) She's the one over there!
Pete Oh, *that* one! Yes—right. (*He laughs, nervously*)
Alan And do you know why she's so nice?
Pete Well, I——
Alan Because she keeps giving me sandwiches! Would *you* like one? (*He holds out the plate of sandwiches*)

Pete What? (*He sees the sandwiches*) Oh. Thanks very much. (*He takes one*)
Sarah And now I'm going to get him some wine.
Jessica He doesn't need wine! He's just leaving!
Pete He can't leave yet. He and George haven't had time for a chat.
Alan (*glaring at George*) No, we haven't! And we've got a lot to talk about.
Haven't we, "old friend"?
George (*surprised by his aggression*) H-have we?
Alan Well, apparently we have something in common.
George Really? Oh, that *is* good news. (*He looks at Pete, apprehensively*)
Sarah Red, wasn't it, Alan?
Alan Yes, please. If it's on the go.
Sarah Right! Red it is. (*She starts to go, but hesitates to whisper to George*)
I think he wants to be your best man.

Sarah nods approvingly, giggles, and goes

*Pete and George are even more confused. Alan advances on George, who
backs a little, nervously*

Alan So, George "old friend"—what makes you think you're going to marry
Jessica?
George (*puzzled*) Jessica?
Alan (*pointing at her*) Jessica!
George I'm not going to marry Jessica! (*Uncertainly*) *Am* I, Jessica?
Jessica Certainly not!
Alan But Sarah said that you and Jessica were——
George (*relaxing, gratefully*) Oh, you mustn't take any notice of Sarah!
She's a bit of a romantic, you see. Always wanting people to be married
to *other* people. Isn't she, Pete?
Pete Well, up to a point…!
Jessica (*to Alan*) You see? What did I tell you?

Alan relaxes, and puts his arm around George cosily. To George's relief

Alan Oh, well, that's all right, then, isn't it? Because if you *had* wanted to
marry her I might have had to kill you. (*He laughs, happily, at the prospect*)
Pete (*amused*) Why should you want to kill George even if he *had* been
married to Jessica?
Alan I'd want to kill *anyone* who was married to Jessica! (*He laughs some
more*)
Pete You—you wouldn't, would you?

Alan starts to lead George towards the garden door

Alan So, George, how's life been treating you since we last met?
George Oh—you know—fairly average...
Alan When *did* we last meet, actually? I seem to have forgotten...

Alan and George continue talking quietly. Jessica pulls Pete aside, urgently, and speaks in anxious hushed tones

Jessica Did you *tell* them?
Pete Who?
Jessica Sarah and her mother! About *us*!
Pete Ah. No. I'm afraid not. Sorry. I know I promised. And I *will* do it, of
   course, but——
Jessica You don't have to!
Pete What?
Jessica Not now.
Pete I thought you wanted me to!
Jessica Yes. I did. But—(*she glances, briefly, towards Alan and George*)—
   not while George's old friend is here.
Pete (*relieved*) Oh. Right. No problem. I won't say a word.
Jessica Thank you, Pete!

Pete is puzzled by Jessica's sudden change of heart

   *Sarah enters with an open bottle of red wine and a glass which she holds
   aloft*

Sarah Red wine for our special guest! (*She goes to Alan and starts to pour
   a glass of wine*)

Alan leans forward and smiles playfully

Alan You got it wrong, didn't you?
Sarah (*looking at the wine*) No. You said red.
Alan George isn't going to marry Jessica!
Sarah How do *you* know?
Alan He *told* me he wasn't.
Sarah (*defiantly*) He *might*...
Alan He *won't*!

   Margot comes in and sees Alan

Margot Good heavens! People keep arriving unexpectedly!
Sarah This is Alan. *He*'s just arrived from *France*!

Margot Whatever for?
Sarah He's a friend of George's.
Margot I didn't know George had friends in France.
George Neither did I...!
Pete And this is Margot. My mother-in-law!
Alan *She* doesn't live here, too, does she?
Pete (*quietly*) No fear...!
Margot (*to Alan*) Are you here for long?
Jessica No! He's just leaving!
Pete He can't leave *now*. He's only just arrived. He hasn't had time to speak to George yet.
Margot You mean you came all the way from France just to speak to George?
Alan (*laughing*) No, no—not *just* to speak to George! I came to collect my girlfriend and take her back to France.
Jessica Well, if you don't go now you'll miss the ferry! (*She tries to urge Alan on his way*)
Margot You mean you've got a girlfriend *here*?
Jessica No, he hasn't!
Alan Yes, he has!
Sarah Is it anyone we know?
Alan Yes, of course! It's Jessica.

They all react

Pete *Jessica*?!
Alan Yes.
Pete (*indicating her*) *This* Jessica?
Alan Yes. *My* Jessica... (*He gazes at her, adoringly*)
Jessica I'm not your Jessica!
Pete You—you mean you've met her before?
Jessica (*to Alan*) You really must go!
Alan Of course I've met her before. We've been living together in France.

They all stare at him in astonishment

Pete Living together in France?!
Alan Yes.
Pete (*to Jessica*) Living together in France?!
Jessica (*rather shamefaced*) Y-yes. I—I'm sorry...

A moment. Then Pete explodes

Pete But we thought you were dead!

Jessica No. I was in France.
Sarah (*puzzled*) *I* thought you were in Tibet...
Jessica I was.
George Climbing a mountain.
Jessica Yes.
Pete And falling off!
Jessica No. Not falling off a mountain. Falling in *love* on a mountain. (*She looks at Alan, lovingly*)
Sarah But what's that got to do with you going to live in France with Alan?
Jessica Because that's where we met.
Sarah (*wide-eyed*) On a mountain in Tibet?
Alan Yes.
Pete So ... So you didn't fall off a mountain at all?
Jessica (*shaking her head in shame*) No...
Margot No wonder you had no lasting injury.
Pete You said you'd lost your memory.
Jessica Yes. I know. I'm so sorry, Pete...
Pete Oh, my God...!
Margot I can't think why *you're* getting so upset about it.
Sarah No. Nor can I. I think it's very romantic. (*Enraptured*) Fancy falling in love on a mountain and then going to live in France... Wonderful...!
Pete It's not wonderful! It's outrageous!
Margot Don't be silly, Pete. For heaven's sake—live and let live!

Pete reacts to her choice of phrase

Pete Yes! Exactly! (*To Jessica again*) You let me and George think that you were dead!
George We even had a memorial service. I made a speech...
Pete And all the time you were having it off with a man on a mountain!
Alan We didn't *stay* on the mountain...
Pete No! You went off to bloody France and lived the life of Riley! (*To Jessica*) If you were still alive you should have telephoned. Or sent a fax. Don't they have fax machines in bloody Tibet?
Sarah Aren't you over-reacting a bit, darling?
Margot Yes, he certainly is! Anyway, how did you and George know about Jessica climbing mountains in the first place?

Pete stares at her, blankly, for a moment

Pete What?
Margot How did you both get to know her?

Another blank stare from Pete. Then George comes to his aid

George We were pen-friends.
Margot Pen-friends?!
Pete (*gratefully*) Yes? Quite right, George. We met her on the internet.
Sarah Then why didn't you know that she and Alan had left Tibet and gone to live in France?

Pete hesitates again

George Because she'd stopped writing, hadn't she?
Pete Yes! Exactly! That's why we assumed that she was dead. We didn't get any more letters.
Sarah That could have been the fault of the Post Office...
Margot You should be delighted to know that poor Jessica is alive and well instead of shouting at everybody.
Jessica Thank you, Margot.
Sarah (*to Alan*) Would you like another sandwich?
Pete No, he wouldn't! He's got no right to come here from France and start drinking my wine and eating my sandwiches!
Margot Really, Pete! What an extraordinary way to behave! Just because you and Jessica were pen-friends doesn't give you the right to dominate her private life.
Sarah (*to Jessica*) And *I* can't understand why you came here today instead of staying in France with Alan.
Alan No! Neither can I!
Sarah (*romantically*) You met him on a mountain—you fell in love—and you went to live in France with him. It was all so romantic... So why did you bother to come back here and look up a couple of old pen-friends?

Pete and George look suitably demeaned

Jessica Because I found out that Alan wasn't only interested in me and mountains but in other women as well! (*She glares at Alan*)
Alan Not other women! *One* other woman!
Jessica And now I don't want to see him ever again!
Sarah Oh, no...! (*Glaring at Alan*) How could you go and spoil such a beautiful romance!

Pete goes across to Jessica, rather hurt by her revelation

Pete So ... was *that* the reason you came here today?
Jessica (*nodding, guiltily*) Yes...
Pete Only because Alan had let you down?
Jessica Yes... (*She lowers her head in shame*)

A moment of silent sadness for Pete. Then...

Pete (*loudly*) Well, that's bloody marvellous! You only turned up here because *he* was after another woman in France!
Alan What the hell has it got to do with you what I do in France?
Margot Yes! You really are being very unreasonable.
Sarah (*to Alan*) I wish now that I'd never given you any sandwiches! How could you treat poor Jessica so badly?
Alan I *didn't* treat her badly.
Jessica Yes, you did!
Alan We lived together for ages!
Jessica Then you went off with another woman!
Alan And came back!
Jessica So you *say*!
Alan And you were just leaving!
Jessica Yes! I was coming back here! (*She glares at Pete*) Where I *thought* I'd be wanted...
Alan I had asked you to marry me, remember!

Pete is frozen. And silent. George turns to him, helpfully

George Did you hear that?
Pete Yes, George! I heard it!

Sarah looks at Alan, her romantic hopes rising

Sarah You ...You asked her to marry you?
Alan Yes. Three times! *Four* times, probably.
Jessica (*to Sarah*) The fourth time he was——
Alan She doesn't need to know that! (*To Sarah*) And each time she said no.
Sarah (*astonished*) She turned you down? (*To Jessica in disbelief*) You ... turned him down?
Jessica Yes...
Sarah Three times? Four times probably?
Jessica Yes...
Sarah Why?!
Alan Thank you, Sarah. That's just what I was going to ask.
Sarah *Why* didn't you marry him, Jessica?
Jessica Because I couldn't!
Sarah Couldn't? Why ever not?
Jessica I couldn't marry *anybody*! Could I, Pete?
Pete Do we have to talk about this now?
Margot What's it got to do with Pete? I thought he was just a pen-friend!

Alan I don't understand. *Why* couldn't you marry me?
Jessica (*loudly*) Because I was already married to Pete!

A dreadful silence. They all turn to stare at Pete in disbelief

Alan She ... she's married to *you*?

Pete nods, a broken man

Pete Yes...
Sarah She can't be!
Pete She *is*.
Jessica I *am*.
Sarah But *I*'m married to Pete! Aren't I, Mummy?
Margot Of course you are!
Sarah (*to Jessica*) George was Pete's best man at our wedding.
Jessica He was at *our* wedding, too...

Another bleak silence. Then Margot explodes

Margot I knew there was something shifty about him! He always had the air of a guilty man...!
Alan (*to Jessica*) So *that* was the reason you turned me down three times, four times probably? Because you were already married!
Jessica Yes, of course! I couldn't have *two* husbands, could I?
Margot Why not? Pete seems to have two wives!
Pete I didn't *know* that, though, did I? *We* thought Jessica had died on a mountain!
Margot And when you thought she was safely out of the way you went in search of pastures new.
Pete It wasn't like that!
George (*helpfully*) No. There *was* a decent time lag...
Pete Thank you, George.
Sarah (*to Jessica*) So after Alan went off with another woman in France you came back here hoping to pick up your life with Pete again?
Jessica (*a little embarrassed*) Well ... Yes. After all, I do still love him. And an *old* husband is better than *no* husband... (*She turns to glare at Pete*) I didn't know then that in my absence, he'd already made other plans!
Pete (*wildly*) But all this time you let me and George think that you were dead so that you could go romping with a mountain climber in France!
Jessica We weren't romping!
Alan Yes, we were. Well, *I* was, anyway.
Jessica (*to Pete*) It's no good you trying to claim the moral high ground. You were the one who got married twice!

Sarah So, Jessica—when you came back here today—you had no idea that
Pete had married again?
Jessica No. It was a *terrible* shock... (*She looks terribly shocked*)

Sarah is immediately sympathetic

Sarah Oh, yes—yes! It must have been. Poor Jessica...! (*She runs across
and embraces her, comfortingly*)

*Jessica reacts uncertainly to this peace-offering, and the others all watch the
cosy get-together in considerable surprise*

Sarah Right! Come on then! (*She takes Jessica's arm, decisively*)
Jessica W-where are we going?
Sarah You and I have got a lot of things to talk about.
Jessica I don't think so...
Sarah Yes! We've got to make a decision.
Jessica Have we?
Sarah Of course! Only *one* of us can be married to Pete.
Jessica Exactly! And Sarah, I do have to tell you that——
Sarah So we'll have to discuss it, won't we?
Jessica But there's nothing to discuss!
Sarah Yes, there is! We've got to come to a decision about Pete.
Pete (*unhappily*) I think Jessica's already *made* a decision...
Sarah Don't be silly, Pete! Jessica and I have got to decide what to do about
you.
Pete *Do* about me?!
Sarah Well, you can't go *on* having two wives, can you? So *we*'ll have to
make up our minds which of us is going to have you and which one isn't.
Pete Don't *I* have any say in the matter?
Sarah Certainly not! You forfeited your right to decide when you married
us both. Come along, Jessica!

Sarah takes Jessica's arm, happily, and leads her out to the kitchen

The others watch them go in astonishment. Alan laughs

Alan Poor old Pete! I wish I'd seen your face when the door opened and your
dead wife walked in!
George Yes, it *was* rather funny...! (*He laughs also*)
Pete George!!

George stops laughing

George Sorry.

Pete drifts in the direction of Alan, feeling rather hurt by his own thoughts

Pete Did ... Did Jessica never mention me at all? When you were both climbing mountains.

Alan (*trying to recall*) No. I don't think so...

Pete My name never cropped up in the conversation?

Alan No...

Pete Not even as a pen-friend?

Alan No...

Margot You could hardly expect to be mentioned. By then Jessica had obviously found other fish to fry! (*She glares at Alan*)

Alan Is *that* what I was? Fried fish?

George Yes! You were fried fish and Sarah was pastures new! (*He laughs*)

Pete George!

George stops laughing

George Sorry.

Alan (*with a sudden thought*) Wait a minute...!

Pete Now what?

Alan If you're still married to Jessica that must mean that your marriage to Sarah is no longer valid.

Pete ⎫
Margot ⎭ (*together*) What?!

Alan So you and Sarah are just an unmarried item.

Margot My daughter is not an item! (*She turns to Pete*) You'll have to divorce Jessica immediately!

Pete I'm not sure if I can...

Margot Of course you can! You can divorce Jessica by naming Alan.

Alan (*outraged*) Why should I be named in her divorce when she never told me she was married?

George I think I've got a *better* idea...

Pete (*warily*) Have you, George?

George Yes! If you aren't really married to Sarah why don't *you* go back to *Jessica*, and *Alan* can marry Sarah?

The others look at George in disapproval

Margot I have no intention of allowing my only daughter to marry a philandering mountain climber from France!

Pete Yes, George. You've gone too far this time

George I was only trying to help ...
Alan Anyway, I don't want to marry Sarah. I want to marry Jessica.

Jessica and Sarah return from their conference

Pete is rather put out by the brevity of their discussion

Pete That didn't take very long.
Jessica No. It was quite easy really. Wasn't it, Sarah?
Sarah Yes.
Pete *Easy?* One of you has got to give me up! That can't be easy!
Jessica Well, it was, actually.
Pete It *was?*
Jessica Certainly.
Sarah Yes.
Pete (*deeply affronted*) *Easy?*! To give up *me?*
Jessica ⎫
            ⎬ (*together*) Yes! (*They smile, happily*)
Sarah ⎭

Pete tries hard to maintain his equilibrium

Pete All right—go on, then! What have you decided?
Sarah Well, you see, the thing is—perhaps you'd better sit down, darling?
Pete As bad as that, is it?
Jessica I think you *ought* to sit down, darling.

Pete sits down, one wife standing on either side of him

   Now I hope you aren't going to be cross and start shouting again.
Pete Why should I start shouting again?
George Yes! After all, whatever you've decided he's still going to end up
   with *one* wife, isn't he? (*He laughs, enjoying the humour of this, until he
   sees Pete's stern face and lets it die*)
Jessica Well, that makes our decision a bit embarrassing. Doesn't it, Sarah?
Sarah It certainly does!

George has another of his inspirations, and grins confidently

George Ah! I bet I know!
Jessica Do you, George?
George Well, I can guess! And that's why you're both embarrassed about
   telling him. You want to share him, don't you?

Pete's two wives exchange a look

Jessica *Share* him?
Sarah (*indicating Pete, disparagingly*) Share *him*?
George (*trying to keep the ball in the air*) Yes! You know—one week on and
one week off. Pete and I discussed it. Didn't we, Pete?

*Pete glares at him, knowing this to be unhelpful. George lets his enthusiasm
die*

Margot (*about to erupt*) You discussed sharing my daughter with another
woman?
George I think you should rephrase that, Margot...
Alan You'd never hear a conversation like this in France!
Margot I'm not staying here to listen to this decadence! Sarah, I suggest you
pack your bags at once and come with *me*—back to normality!

Margot storms out

Pete puts on a brave face and tries to remain optimistic

Pete Well, come on, then! Which of you has won the jackpot?

Jessica looks at Sarah with a weary smile

Jessica You'd better tell him, Sarah.
Sarah Yes. Right. (*She hesitates*)
Pete Well, come on! What have you decided?
Sarah We've decided ... that *neither* of us wants to be your wife.

Pete freezes for a moment unable to believe his ears

Pete *Neither* of you?!
George I didn't think *that* choice was on the agenda...
Jessica Well, that's what we've decided. I'm going to get divorced and go
back to France—with Alan—(*she looks at him*)—provided he still wants
to *marry* me.
Alan I certainly do!
Sarah And I'm going to be a single woman again.

Pete gets up and stares at her, appalled

Pete You can't suddenly decide to be a single woman again! Can she,
George?
George Wouldn't have thought so.

Sarah Yes, I can.
Pete But you're my wife!
Sarah Not any more. You're still married to Jessica.
Pete Yes, I suppose I am... (*He looks at Jessica, helplessly*)

Jessica goes to him with a small sad smile

Jessica Oh, Pete ... I'm sorry I gave you such a shock coming back from the dead like that. And I do love you... (*She gives him a brief, fond kiss*) But I love Alan, too! And *he*'s not married! (*She runs back to Alan*)
Alan I soon *will* be!

Alan and Jessica embrace, happily. Pete looks on, mournfully

George, old friend...
George (*fearful of another painful embrace*) Y-yes?
Alan I've got a great idea!
George (*apprehensively*) You haven't, have you?
Alan When Jessica and I *do* get married how about you being my best man?

George hesitates, out of loyalty to Pete

George Oh, I don't know about that. I've never been a best man in France.
Pete Anyway, that's quite out of the question! If *anyone*'s going to be Alan's best man when he marries my wife it'll be *me*!
Alan (*with a big smile*) You're on!

Jessica and Alan go out happily into the hall

Pete sinks on to the sofa in despair. George hovers, uncertainly, embarrassed by the situation

George Whisky?
Pete It's too late now for whisky!

Sarah looks at Pete and smiles, innocently

Sarah What's the matter, darling?
Pete What's the matter?! A moment ago I'd got *two* wives, now I've got none! (*He gets up and wanders away a little, deeply despondent*) So ...So where will you be living, then?
Sarah When?
Pete From now on!

George (*helpfully*) You can use *my* house if you like and I'll move in with Pete until you've decided where you're going.
Sarah But I'm not going anywhere.

Pete and George exchange a puzzled look

Pete You aren't?
Sarah No. I'll still be living here. (*She smiles, happily*)
George Oh, I don't think that's on the agenda, not now you're a single woman again.
Pete George—leave this to me.
George Oh. Yes. Right.
Pete (*to Sarah*) I thought you said you were leaving me?
George Yes, that's what *I* thought...

Pete glares at him

Sorry.
Pete Isn't that what you said?
Sarah No. I didn't say *that*!
Pete You didn't?
Sarah No.
George *I* thought she did...
Pete George...!
George Sorry.
Pete (*to Sarah*) What *did* you say, then?
Sarah I said I was going to be a single woman again. I'll still be living here with you, only we won't be a married couple any more.
George (*turning to Pete*) Oh, I'm not sure about that...

He stops as Pete gives him a look

Sorry...
Sarah (*getting back into romantic mode*) Oh, Pete! It'll be so romantic! I'll be a single woman living with a married man! We'll be an item!

Pete laughs, happy and relieved, and holds out his arms to her

Sarah runs towards him, but trips and nearly falls

Sarah Oooh!
Pete Careful! (*He catches her in time*)

George rushes to assist

George Are you all right?
Sarah I'm not sure. Perhaps this time I really *have* sprained my ankle!
Pete Well, don't tell your mother or she'll stay and bandage it all over again!
George (*helpfully*) Perhaps I should prepare a poultice?
Sarah (*laughing*) No. George—it's all right—really!
Pete Well, you definitely need bedrest.
George No question of it!
Pete And *I'll* make some soup. Come along, George! We'd better carry her upstairs so she can have a lie-down.

They pick Sarah up, despite her giggling protestations

Sarah No, no! Don't be silly! I can lie down here on the sofa!
Pete No, you can't! If you're a single woman living in the house of a married man you'll do as you're told. Come on, George!

Margot comes in, ready to leave, and sees them. She reacts in horror at the sight of Sarah in the arms of two men

Margot *Now* what's going on?! What are you doing with my daughter?
Pete George—what are we doing with her daughter?
George (*with a big smile*) Taking her up to bed, of course!
Margot *Both* of you?!
Pete Well, he was my best man!

Appalled by such decadence, Margot departs in haste towards the front door

Realizing that Margot has misunderstood their intentions, Pete and Sarah and George collapse on to the sofa, laughing helplessly

Black-out

THE END

FURNITURE AND PROPERTY LIST

Further dressing may be added at the director's discretion

ACT I

On stage: Sofa
Sofa table. *On it:* magazine
Table. *On it:* telephone, tin of biscuits
Drinks table. *On it:* whisky, 4 glasses
Desk. *On it:* framed photograph of Sarah

Off stage: Wrapped bottle of wine, laptop computer, evening paper (**Pete**)
Handbag containing bandage, scissors (**Margot**)
Handbag containing powder compact (**Jessica**)
Aspirins (**Margot**)
Open bottle of champagne, 3 glasses (**George**)

Personal: **Pete**: wrist-watch, mobile phone
George: handkerchief, latchkey

ACT II

On stage: As before

Off stage: Plate of sandwiches (**Sarah**)
Open bottle of red wine, wine glass (**Sarah**)

Personal: **Pete**: George's key

LIGHTING PLOT

Property fittings required: nil
1 interior. The same throughout

ACT I

To open: Sunny summer evening interior lighting

Cue 1	**Pete** sinks on to the sofa *Black-out*	(Page 43)

ACT II

To open: Sunny summer evening interior lighting

Cue 2	**Pete, Sarah** and **George** collapse on to the sofa *Black-out*	(Page 84)

EFFECTS PLOT

ACT I

ACT II

No cues